THE BUSINESS
OF HEDGING

THE BUSINESS
OF HEDGING

Sound Risk Management
without the Rocket-Science

John J. Stephens

FINANCIAL TIMES
Prentice Hall

An imprint of Pearson Education

London • New York • San Francisco • Toronto • Sydney • Tokyo • Singapore
Hong Kong • Cape Town • Madrid • Amsterdam • Munich • Paris • Milan

PEARSON EDUCATION LIMITED

Head Office:
Edinburgh Gate
Harlow CM20 2JE
Tel: +44 (0)1279 623623
Fax: +44 (0)1279 431059

London Office:
128 Long Acre
London WC2E 9AN
Tel: +44 (0)20 7447 2000
Fax: +44 (0)20 7240 5771
Website: www.business-minds.com

———————————————

First published in Great Britain in 2000

© Pearson Education Limited 2000

The right of John J. Stephens to be identified as Author
of this Work has been asserted by him in accordance
with the Copyright, Designs and Patents Act 1988.

ISBN 0 273 65203 6

British Library Cataloguing in Publication Data
A CIP catalogue record for this book can be obtained from the British Library

Library of Congress Cataloging in Publication Data
Applied for.

10 9 8 7 6 5 4 3 2

Typeset by Northern Phototypesetting Co. Ltd, Bolton
Printed and bound by Bell & Bain Ltd, Glasgow

The Publishers' policy is to use paper manufactured from sustainable forests.

THE AUTHOR

John Stephens lives with his wife in the suburbs to the west of Johannesburg, South Africa. A graduate of the university of the Witwatersrand, John practiced law in Johannesburg for 22 years. For 10 years afterwards he served as CEO of a business-consulting firm. He has acted as Financial Advisor to some major financial institutions and, most recently, he has been developing and conducting seminars for training staff in financial risk management. He studied the theory and practice of risk management with financial derivatives in the USA and the UK. He has lived at various times in London, Chicago and Miami. John is presently a non-executive director of a UK based Web software development firm and spends at least three months a year in London. He acts as risk management consultant to companies, writes books on financial subjects and regularly contributes articles to international periodicals. He also acts as keynote speaker and seminar leader. John can be contacted by e-mail at futurae@icon.co.za or futurae@hotmail.com

With affection –
To Philip, who made it all possible; and
to Annalie, who started it off.

TABLE OF CONTENTS

PREFACE

Every day, after the close of business, your premises are locked up aren't they? Every day, before you go home, you make sure that your office is in order – that important documents are locked away, that the safe is closed and locked. Somebody checks that all the faucets in the bathrooms and kitchen areas are closed to prevent an overnight flood. The last person to leave makes sure that the fire and burglar alarms are set. Every day you, or some other responsible person, makes sure that your business, your factory, or whatever, is locked tight, safe and protected from harm. It just wouldn't make sense to leave everything for anybody to walk in and help themselves to your valuable assets, cash, documents and other things, would it? It wouldn't be wise to leave faucets open, hotplates on and other machinery running. There's no telling what damage could result if one weren't ever vigilant on these matters.

But have you locked the door on the ravages of changing interest rates? And what about the value of the currency that you have to trade in every day? Have you protected its value for you in your business? Have you protected your business against a drop in the value of its assets due to changing comodity prices? Have you checked that the gushing faucets of rising cost and declining markets aren't flushing your profits down the drain while you're dreaming away? If you cannot answer yes to all these questions, then right now, your business is leaking at the seams. As you read this it is leaking money – your money or your job. The knowledge in this book will help you to really lock your business up; it will show you how to set the alarms and how to get it financially watertight. That is what the business of hedging is all about.

The idea for this book arose from quite unexpected circumstances. After more than two decades practising law and then business consulting, I spent some time during 1997 in the US and the UK studying derivatives. During this period, I came to appreciate what a potent and essential technique hedging is for every business in every industry. I was later to discover that financial hedging is also a lost art and a neglected craft for most people engaged in business. It just does not form part of their consciousness and it is not part of their lives.

Upon my return to my home in South Africa, I developed a course on hedging for people engaged in the agricultural industry. I still present this course in two-day seminars in addition to my business consulting. In the course of these activities, I consulted with many clients and discussed the business of hedging with them. To my considerable surprise at the time, I discovered that they did not hedge away any of their business risk. And not only did they not hedge in their businesses, they knew virtually nothing about derivatives.

Some clients vaguely recalled the Barings Bank debacle. They all seemed to recall that the disaster had resulted from some bright spark trading commodity futures in Singapore. That single piece of information apparently summed up their total knowledge of derivatives. The considered consensus was that it was territory fit only for gamblers. What great business opportunities were being missed, I thought at the time.

As may well be expected, people who lack information and do not understand a subject cannot work up any enthusiasm for it. I consequently endeavoured to obtain some literature on hedging. I wanted these people to read about the business and to get up to speed on the subject. Although there were numerous books dealing with derivatives, most of which touched on the subject of hedging to some degree, I failed to find anything suitable. Virtually all the literature was aimed at the banking and financial sectors. A mass of advanced academic literature was also available, obviously intended for the academic, professional and advanced practitioner rather than the businessperson, who might find it somewhat perplexing.

Inquiries among my friends and acquaintances in the US revealed that in their experience, very few small to medium-sized businesses outside of agriculture make use of hedging. Agriculture is an exception to the rule because it is the cradle of derivative instruments.

The earliest known derivative instruments were developed for agricultural purposes. It is a well-recorded fact that the Ancient Greeks used options as financial instruments in agriculture many years BC. The legal principles and rules relating to options and forward contracts were generally established in Roman law by the time of the Emperor Justinian circa 500AD. In ancient times, these types of contractual arrangements were thus widely employed. Later, after the final collapse of the western Roman Empire, they were perpetuated in the laws of all European nations.

In modern times, the futures contract was born out of the forward contract. This is dealt with in the body of this book. It is therefore not surprising to find that there are many knowledgeable farmers, elevator operators, feed-lot operators, millers and such who would never dream of doing business if they were not fully hedged at all times. In fact, the free market system would be unthinkable, not to mention unworkable, without the use of derivatives. In the broader world economy, the financial gurus, the whiz kids, stockbrokers and the people running big business know all about it – they use hedging daily. Banks and financial institutions would be unable to survive without derivatives and hedging. Yet it appears that the full benefits of these instruments and markets have never quite reached through to the ordinary businessperson.

What was required, in my opinion, was a good 'how to' book that started from the fundamentals and assumed no knowledge on the part of the reader. The business of hedging ought then to be systematically and clearly explained to a point where the reader would be self-sufficient in the marketplace.

Hence, I started putting together this book. In doing so it was my intention to bring together all the basic information on the business of hedging in a simple and uncomplicated manner. My first purpose is to deal with the subject in such a way that businesspeople who know nothing or very little of the business of hedging will gain an overall understanding of the subject. In the process, I trust that they will begin to appreciate how hedging will add value to their businesses. Second, if you are such a businessperson, I wish to impart sufficient information to you to enable you to use basic hedging techniques successfully in your business. Hedging is, after all, only a technique. To be both useful and successful it needs to be understood, learned and practised.

I have often heard the objection that in order to use hedging one needs to be an expert at reading and calling the market. I wish to state categorically that this perception is false. The hedger goes to the market for protection precisely because he does not know what the market is going to do. The hedger is there to protect the business from the vagaries of the market. The moment a person takes a view on how the market is going to perform and takes a position accordingly, that person is not engaged in hedging but in speculating. That is a totally different business, which falls out of the scope of this book.

Although to practise the techniques of hedging you require a basic understanding of how the markets operate, it is quite unnecessary to have an exhaustive understanding of all the market forces and mechanisms that are at work. The only essential knowledge of the marketplace is the knowledge that you already have to run your business successfully, plus the knowledge you will gain from this book. The knowledge and understanding of hedging imparted herein will be built on to your existing knowledge base. From my experience in lecturing these techniques to farmers and people engaged in the agricultural industry, I know that this can be achieved. Any person who is competent enough to run a business can grasp and use these techniques effectively.

Part One of this book is consequently devoted to explaining the foundations of hedging. How you should evaluate risk in your business and how hedging deals with the risk are fundamentally explained. Part Two deals with the tools of hedging – derivatives. The technical aspects of all relevant derivative instruments are explained, and we look at how the exchange-traded derivatives work and how you should approach their use. The functioning of exchanges and how the prices of exchange-traded derivatives relate to the cash markets are fully discussed.

Part Three sets out to explain in detail the basic strategies of hedging. The principles are demonstrated by means of exercises and examples of business problems encountered in the real world. The explanations are not academic; they illustrate the sort of situations you might encounter in your business. Their purpose is to show you how to identify the risk pitfalls and the hedging opportunities in your business and how you should deal with them. At the same time, it demonstrates all the basic hedging techniques that have played, and continue to play, such a vital role in the success of so many businesses throughout the world.

The ultimate purpose in writing this book is to assist you, the reader, in gaining wider horizons for your business. If these efforts allow you to expand your business, or add value to it, they will all have been worthwhile. So, if you are new to the business of hedging, I hope this will be a pleasant and ultimately rewarding journey of discovery. Even if you are not totally new to the subject, I sincerely hope and trust that you will profit from some of the ideas traversed herein. Therefore, it remains only for me to wish you *bon voyage*!

PART ONE

Foundations of Hedging Financial Risk

CHAPTER ONE

The Background to Hedging

Why Hedging is Your Business

The business of hedging is everybody's business. Businesses are continuously exposed to risks from various sources. The purpose of hedging is to neutralize, or actually to offset, certain risks in a business. It follows that hedging, in one way or another, must form part of the business plan of every business.

Consider the fact that the price of gold is quite volatile. It takes two years and a tremendous amount of capital to bring a gold mine into production. How can anybody pour so much money into such a project without any certainty of what the price of gold is going to be when the mine starts producing? Have you ever wondered how banks and building societies manage to give long-term mortgages at fixed rates, while they borrow short term at floating interest rates? Both of these questions have the same simple answer: mining houses and banks are in the business of hedging.

Hedging really is for everybody. It is not only of benefit to those businesses that traditionally make use of hedging. With the dramatic explosion of the ideas of risk management and the increase in availability of derivative instruments, hedging has become a very real tool in the hands of every business. As you read this, new hedging opportunities are arising somewhere. It may be just the opportunity you have always needed to boost your bottom line, or to beat the daylights out of the competition.

Identifying Risks in an Enterprise

Some risks are inherent to the enterprise itself. For example, the most basic inherent risk of a shoe merchant is that people will not continue to buy shoes. Other risks are not inherent but are overlaid on to inherent risk. Such risks are voluntarily assumed, such as those associated with a particular marketing strategy. Using the shoe merchant again, should he decide to market shoes by opening a retail shop, he then runs the additional risk of location. The risk is that, assuming people continue to buy shoes, they might not buy shoes at the particular place where this shop is located.

There are, of course, a number of areas in a business that give rise to financial risk. For example, when you start a business, the first thing that happens is that you invest money. It may be your own money, shareholders' money, borrowed money or any combination of these. Whichever it is, money remains the basic raw material of your business and its constantly changing price is one of the risks that you face. As Ciaran Walsh says, in his book 'Key Management Ratios', FT Prentice Hall 1996: 'Enterprises that *continue* to earn a return sufficient to pay the market rate for funds usually prosper. Those enterprises that fail over a considerable period to meet this going market rate usually do not survive – at least in the same form and under the same leadership.'

There are a number of other risks and sources of risk. During the course of the discussions contained in this book, I will constantly attempt to show how risks and their sources may be discovered and identified. Identifying the basic risks in your business is your first priority. Not all risks are immediately obvious – some are very subtle and others are well hidden. When they do reveal themselves however, their effects can be devastating.

Many sources of risk abound in the economy in which we operate. Virtually all the market forces that interplay on the world economic stage are also evident in local markets. The forces that are active in a nation's economy at any given moment are also active in the derivatives and the equity markets. These forces are a source of risk for every business in the economy.

Both general economic factors, that impact only on certain sectors of the economy, and other factors that are peculiar to your specific business interplay to put your financial wellbeing in jeopardy. The business of hedging has as its purpose the analysis and discovery of those factors that put your business at risk. Once that has been achieved, the best possible way of neutralising those risks through using the derivatives markets can be identified.

By means of the examples quoted throughout this book, it is hoped that you will look at your business anew and ask yourself what risks you really face. Only then will you be able to quantify the risk, allowing you to take the necessary remedial action through hedging.

Risk and Reward

Business risks are those factors that threaten profit in the business. The purpose of business is to make a profit and a profit can only be a profit if it sounds in money. When we refer to risks therefore, we refer to risks that sound in money. To put it differently, we wish to concern ourselves with those aspects of risk that can be quantified in monetary terms.

Risk and business are thus two sides of the same coin. And since they are inextricably bound, it follows that risk is not a bad thing to be avoided at all costs. On the contrary, without risk there would probably be no reward.

Managing Risk and Hedging Risk

Risk that is not managed properly has the capacity to destroy the very business of which it is such an inseparable concomitant. However, managing risk and hedging risk are not the same thing.

The purpose of risk management is, at its broadest sweep, to identify all the risks in a business, to quantify them and then to manage them. The underlying idea is that the business manager must remain in control of the risk and not vice versa. Managing risk therefore does not necessarily mean getting rid of it, although it may require getting rid of some of it, but a lot of the risk has to be managed in such a way that the business obtains maximum reward from the risks run.

The purpose of hedging, on the other hand, is to neutralize selected risks in a business. Clearly, then, hedging is part and parcel of risk management, but it is primarily aimed at offsetting unavoidable, unwanted risk in a business.

Avoidable but Desired Risk

We stated earlier that risk and profit are concomitants. Indeed, one would seldom expect to find a profit opportunity that carries no risk, although there are, of course, such opportunities. They follow from price discrepancies in the marketplace and arbitrageurs take advantage of them. We will deal with them when we discuss pricing in the marketplace.

To illustrate what is meant by avoidable risk that is yet desired, let us consider the following example. Imagine a roulette wheel with only 36 numbers but which has no zero or double zero. Half the numbers are red and the other half are black. If a bet is placed on red, the risk is that a black number will come up. If a bet is placed on black, the risk is that a red number will come up. There is an even chance of either colour coming up. Therefore, if the payout is 1–1 for a bet on either colour, the risk/reward profile is balanced.

This risk of placing a bet on any one colour can be hedged by placing an equal bet on the other colour. There is then no risk of loss, but equally, there is no opportunity for gain. Playing the game would be pointless. The risk that is assumed by betting on any one colour is therefore an avoidable but desired risk. Given the purpose of taking the risk in the first instance, one would not hedge it.

Unavoidable and Undesired Risk

Examples of risk that is both unavoidable and undesired would be the financial risk of the death of key employees in a business, or the risk of damage to goods and equipment. Life insurance would give protection against the former and short-term all-risks or catastrophe insurance against the latter.

Since we are all mortals, the risk of mortality is unavoidable. However, since it is not from a key person's mortality that a business derives value, it is an unwanted and unproductive risk. Obviously, one cannot protect a business from a person's death, but one can protect the business from most of the financial consequences of mortality. By buying protection against the risk, the business gains financial security and loses no profitability. The same considerations apply to the risk of damage to goods and equipment.

As we will see in later chapters, there is only a slight difference between hedging risk and buying insurance against risk. Strictly speaking, hedging is the voluntary assumption of a risk to neutralize another risk. One can argue with some force that in buying insurance, one risks the loss of the premium if the term of the insurance ends before a claim arises. When we deal with the subject of options, it will become clear that buying options and buying insurance are the same thing in principle. The major difference, however, is that an option has a value that fluctuates with market conditions, while pure insurance policies do not have any value.

Conclusion

Two points emerge from the discussion thus far. First, one obviously does not neutralize avoidable risk – one avoids it, or one assumes it on purpose in order to gain a particular advantage. Second, one does not neutralize desired risk. Desired risk is intended risk that must be there in order for an enterprise to function profitably.

Hedging is a particular technique of neutralizing risk. It is an extremely flexible and powerful technique that allows user firms to concentrate on their core business, while removing the threat of incidental risk.

CHAPTER TWO

The Fundamentals

The Nature of a Financial Hedge

At the most basic level a hedge can be said to be a risk that is intentionally taken in order to offset another risk. It follows that the risk entailed in a hedge is both avoidable and desired. The risk that it offsets must be both unavoidable and undesired.

A risk can hedge another risk only if it is qualitatively opposite and quantitatively equal to that other risk. Another way of putting it is that the hedging risk must be negatively correlated with the risk that it hedges.

Negative Correlation

Correlation is a term that originates from probability theory and relies on statistical analysis but is often estimated from historical data. It is a measure of the extent to which two random variables tend to track one another. The correlation can range from perfectly negative through totally uncorrelated to perfectly positive. Quantitatively, it is expressed as a value ranging from −1 to 1.

In order to demonstrate a perfectly negative correlation, let us analyze our game of roulette that we imagined in the previous chapter. The qualitative risk, when betting on red, is that the wheel will come up with a number that is 'not red'. A $10 bet on red will result in a quantitative risk of $10. Since on our imaginary wheel the only possibility other than red is black, the qualitative risk of the bet on black will be that the wheel will come up with a number that is 'not black'. Since 'not black' = red, and 'not red' = black, it is clear that the two risks are qualitatively opposite. If $10 is wagered on red and $10 wagered on black at the same time by the same person, the quantitative risks are equal. It is clear that the two risks track one another perfectly – if the outcome is not red, it is black. The bet on red is completely nullified by the bet on black. It is a perfect hedge and the two risks have a negative correlation. In this case the correlation is a perfect −1.

Risks can be mathematically equated to vectors. A vector is a certain magnitude of force that works in a particular direction. Figure 2.1 illustrates the roulette wheel example, with the two risks shown as vectors (arrows), working in opposite directions with equal force (indicated by the length of the arrows).

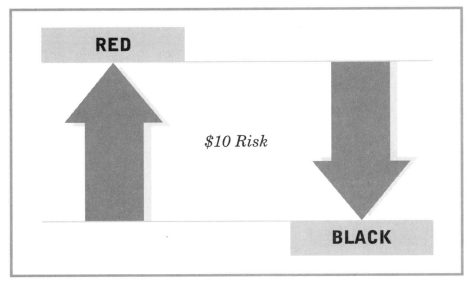

**Figure
2.1**

A perfect hedge

If the two bets were not quantitatively equal, they would obviously not cancel one another out. Thus, if the bet on red were larger than the bet on black, it would have the same effect as a sole bet on red for the difference. This is illustrated by Fig. 2.1 in which the two vector forces of risk cancel one another out. If the arrows pointed in the same direction, the risk would be doubled or leveraged. If the arrows were at 90° relative to each other, they would be uncorrelated.

To demonstrate a further point, let us now assume that the roulette wheel is a regulation French one. That means that because of the zero, there are now 37 numbers, of which one (the zero) is neither red nor black. The bet on red and the one on black are no longer qualitatively equal. The risks do not track one another perfectly any more and incidentally, if you were to place an equal bet on red and black at the same time, there would only be a chance of loss and none of gain.

This simple example demonstrates that if the performance of risk 'A' is to track the performance of risk 'B' both totally and negatively, it necessarily implies a relationship between them, as illustrated in Table 2.1. The table indicates that when one risk gains in value, the other must lose value. Also, the respective gain and loss must be equal in value, while they must take place contemporaneously.

In real life it would be extremely difficult, not to say impossible, to find two risks which correlate so precisely. However, using the proper tools, risks with such correlations can be constructed.

Risk A		Risk B	
Time Period C	Gains one value point	**Time Period C**	Loses one value point
	Loses one value point		Gains one value point

Table 2.1

A correlation of –1 between two risks

Positively Correlated Risks

For the record, we can note that there are two other ways in which random risks may be correlated. First, risks may be positively correlated. They are positively correlated when their respective performances tend to track each other directly, i.e. when the one gains in value, so does the other, and vice versa. The more closely they track each other, the higher the correlation. Risks that are positively correlated leverage each other. That has the effect of substantially increasing the risk. You must never lose sight of this danger. In an attempt to hedge one risk, care must be taken not to leverage another.

Uncorrelated Risks

Second, risks may be completely uncorrelated. This means that their outcomes are not in any way related to each other. They move at random and any similarity in outcomes will be completely co-incidental. Uncorrelated risks diversify one another. Because they move totally at random with respect to each other, they tend to dampen each other's risk. Their returns, however, are not dampened. In other words, the expected return on two uncorrelated risks are cumulative, but their cumulative risk is less than the sum of the two individual risks. Diversification is a risk management tool but does not form part of the business of hedging.

Correlation and Mathematics

The exact correlation between any two variables can be mathematically calculated. The normal formula incorporates the values, expected values and volatilities of the variables. Because of the instruments and techniques discussed in this book, you will not be required to calculate correlations in order to use the basic hedging techniques successfully in your business. There is a wealth of reading matter on this subject if you are interested in reading up on the mathematics.

Essential Elements of a Financial Hedge

From the discussion so far we are able to demonstrate the essential elements of a financial hedge. A hedge is a risk taken with the express purpose of offsetting another risk. In order for one risk to offset another risk, the two risks must be negatively correlated. Their changes in value must be equal, opposite in direction and contemporaneous. This necessitates that when one variable appreciates by a certain amount, the other must depreciate by a like amount at the same time.

The Need to Measure Risk

Since there must be a quantitative correlation between a hedging risk and the risk being hedged, it follows that both risks must be measured in some way. Consequently, a number of methods have been developed to measure risk.

It bears repeating at this stage that this book is not concerned with portfolio management. It is also not written with the professional trader, portfolio manager or asset manager in mind. Virtually all the studies, analyzes and developments that have been made regarding risk-measuring tools and techniques have been done to assist professional portfolio managers. While great strides have been made, most of that effort has provided very little of value to the ordinary businessperson.

Having said that, we must also realize that measuring risk is never irrelevant. It is a matter that every risk-taker must keep in mind at all times. The risk-taker must ask: 'How much risk am I taking?' Put differently, the risk-taker must know how much money can be lost on the venture. It is therefore essential that we deal with the question of measuring risk. Because in most businesses the manager is usually not faced with a complex basket of financial variables to control, measuring the risk is much simpler. Nevertheless, it will be of value for every person in business to have some grasp of what these risk-measuring techniques are about. After discussing the most prominent risk-measuring tools, we shall identify and discuss those risks that concern us in the business of hedging.

Volatility as a Measure of Risk

Volatility is the most basic of all statistical measurements of risk. Any measurement that is subject to random variation has volatility. Volatility tells us how easily the values can change and by how much they are apt to change. One can take virtually any value as an example.

Take a measurement of the ambient temperature in your living room at exactly 12 noon for the next week, or even the next month.

Whatever the time of year, you will probably find that the temperature is virtually never exactly the same. Then draw a graph of your measurements. Draw an x-axis representing the period over which you took the measurements and divide it into equal segments, each representing one day. The y-axis is measured out to reflect temperature. Plot the temperatures for each day against the x- and y-axis. A zigzag pattern will emerge. That zigzag pattern represents the volatility of that week's or that month's noon temperature in your living room.

Draw two parallel horizontal lines so that the upper line intersects the point of the highest temperature and the lower one intersects the point of the lowest temperature. The distance between the lines will give you the volatility parameters of the temperature in your living room. The further the lines are apart, the higher the volatility, and vice versa. Statistically, however, it is necessary to quantify volatility by giving it a numerical value.

In financial analysis, the volatility of a variable value is typically quantified as being the standard deviation of that variable. Volatility therefore tells us by how much the value of an asset can randomly vary over a given period of time. It is numerically expressed as a percentage of the expected value of the variable over the stated period.

What Volatility Tells Us

In practice then, volatility can provide a partial answer to the investor's perennial question: 'How much can I lose (or gain) if I make this investment now?' The reply given by the volatility estimate of that investment tells us by how much the value can stray over a given period. Assume for the moment that the investment in question is a stock with an annual volatility rating of 18 per cent. This might be interpreted as meaning that, over a typical year, the value of the stock will stray by around 18 per cent from its anticipated year-end value. The answer to the initial query might then be something like: 'Well, if the bottom doesn't drop out of the market, you probably won't lose more than 18 per cent of the anticipated value. You probably won't gain more than 18 per cent of the anticipated value either.' The actual value will be within 18 per cent of the value you expect at the end of the year.

What the anticipated value is, is of course an issue not statistically determined. It is not the statistically expected value but rather a value that a particular investor or analyst might anticipate, given economic circumstances, market reactions, management, new products, competition and any other set of inputs. For example, an analyst might state that he anticipates that a particular stock might appreciate from $14.45 to $21.20 by the end of the year. Even assuming the correctness of his analysis, the volatility of that particular stock suggests that the actual price may stray up, or down, from this anticipated value by the indicated percentage.

High and Low Volatility

Obviously, the higher the volatility, the greater the variation of value, and therefore the greater the risk. Also, be warned, volatility is itself a variable. The volatilities of many financial variables, such as stock prices, interest rates, commodities and asset portfolios, are calculated on a daily basis. Certain economic factors that relate to a particular equity or to a particular commodity will influence its price and/or its volatility. From time to time, economic factors and political decisions will influence the volatility of all financial variables. Their effects can be felt throughout the financial markets of a country or a group of countries, or they may affect markets worldwide. Figure 2.2 illustrates how low and high volatility in company stocks might show in a price graph. It demonstrates how the values of two particular financial variables, e.g. the prices of two stocks, might vary over a period of time. It is clear that holding the equity depicted on the right involves greater financial risk than holding the equity depicted on the left.

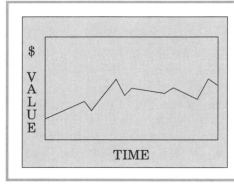 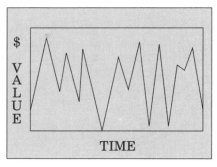

Figure 2.2

Low and high volatility in company stocks

Historic Volatility

The volatility of any financial variable is generally estimated based on the recent fluctuations in value of that variable. The volatility of the gold price may be estimated from the fluctuations in the spot market price of the metal over the past 20 trading days, the past 100 trading days, or over the past year. The estimate based on the data for each period will probably give a different result. The usefulness of each estimate will depend on the purpose for which the risk needs to be measured.

As you can see, historical volatility estimates are highly versatile and flexible. They are not only useful to measure the risk of a particular instrument, or commodity, but they can be used to determine the risk of a whole portfolio of mixed assets. A portfolio is actually a basket of assets and instruments, each with its own risk profile. In order for the volatility of a whole portfolio to be estimated, the only condition is that historical data must be available for that portfolio, as constituted.

Limitations of Volatility as a Measure of Risk

Notwithstanding the advantages, there are also serious shortcomings in volatility as a measure of risk. Since it is based on historical data, the estimate might say very little about how risky the investment is today. Its most serious shortcomings are in measuring the riskiness of a portfolio. In addition, for investors whose portfolios are constantly changing because of their trading activity, historical estimates are less than useful. They do not tell them how volatile the continuously reconstituted portfolio is, or how its market risk will change if particular assets are sold and others are bought.

As asset and portfolio management developed, better and better measures of risk were required. Many different measures have been developed and each has its use. One of the best for portfolios is the so-called 'value at risk', or VAR. Because it incorporates other measures of risk into its estimate, it fills many of the lacunae left by other risk measures. VAR measures the immediate riskiness of a portfolio, which the volatility estimate cannot do. Yet it is based on the historical volatitilities of the individual assets held in the portfolio. In addition, it takes into account how the different variables in the portfolio are correlated. We shall now examine this measure more closely.

Measuring the Value at Risk (VAR)

This measurement is used to estimate the market risk of a portfolio for which historical price data does not exist. VAR is also variously referred to as 'dollars at risk', 'capital at risk', or 'earnings at risk'. However it might be termed, the technical definition remains the same:

'The value at risk is an amount of money, such that the portfolio will lose less than that amount over a specified period with a specified probability.'

A very actively traded portfolio would have its VAR estimated over a short period, e.g. a one-day period with a 97 per cent probability. It might be expressed as $550,000, one-day, 97 per cent. This means that the portfolio is expected to lose less than $550,000 for 97 days out of every 100. The estimate would be based on the portfolio's current composition and recent market behaviour. If it were taken over a longer period, the same portfolio's VAR could be expressed as $2,300,000, one-month, 94 per cent. This means that the portfolio will lose less than $2,300,000 for 94 months out of every 100.

Estimating a portfolio's VAR is a rather challenging exercise but an extremely powerful measure of risk. All the sources of market risk relating to all assets that contribute to the profitability-probability distribution are encompassed in the estimate. Practically speaking, the methodology is to systematize the analysis. A database of volatility and correlation estimates for all the variables that might affect a portfolio is built and maintained. A computer is then able to track the holdings of the portfolio, providing up-to-date VAR estimates as the portfolio is traded.

While theoretically all sources of market risk are encapsulated in VAR, various methods are used to do the estimates. Each method has its advantages and its limitations.

Closed Form Value at Risk

The closed form model assumes that the portfolio for which the estimate is being done has profitability that is normally distributed. A normal distribution refers to a mathematical function of probability. A bell-shaped curve graphically defines a normal probability distribution.

The second assumption is that the profitability depends on the applicable risk factors linearly. It is for this reason that the closed form model is also referred to as 'linear', 'parametric' or 'delta-normal' value at risk. Given these assumptions, the VAR can be calculated directly from the volatilities and correlations of all the risk factors as they may apply to the financial variables included in the portfolio.

For portfolios that conform to these two assumptions, the VAR estimates produced by this model will be exact. Portfolios for which this model can be successfully employed are those that are made up of equities, short-term debt instruments such as commodity positions, or US Treasury bills, whether in the spot or futures markets. The spot and futures markets will be examined in detail in due course.

Limitations of Closed Form VAR

Portfolios that do not conform to the two basic assumptions, such as those that contain options, cannot be analyzed by means of this model. As we will see when we deal with options, their values are not connected linearly to their risk factors but by convexity. Such portfolios are therefore said to have 'convexity' or 'gamma'.

Monte Carlo Value at Risk

The Monte Carlo method is the only one that can produce precise results for the VAR of complex portfolios. The technique employed by this method is to construct a histogram of possible profits and losses for that portfolio over a specified period of time. The construction of such a histogram is also referred to as a simulation. This particular simulation of profits and losses is called the Monte Carlo simulation. The histogram is then used to estimate the VAR of the portfolio.

Although this technique virtually eliminates the model risk associated with other methods, it is extremely difficult to implement. Even a high-speed computer takes a long time to perform the simulation.

Volatility Measurement Versus VAR

In the discussion up to this point we have dealt with the major techniques of risk measurement. We have discussed the fact that all variables have volatility and that this was the basic measurement of their risk. The volatility of a value is merely its standard deviation. The standard deviation of any variable can easily be calculated from its historical changes in value.

We have also noted that the greatest shortcoming of volatility estimates is that they do not give an accurate measure of risk for portfolios. Portfolios contain a basket of risks. Unless there is a reasonable amount of historical price data for the portfolio as presently constituted, volatility cannot give an adequate measure of its risk.

For actively traded portfolios, a value at risk or VAR estimate is more appropriate. We have discussed two methodologies for determining VAR, the closed form VAR and the Monte Carlo simulation. The former method is precise for portfolios with normally distributed profitability and containing financial variables that are linearly connected to their risk factors. For complex portfolios or portfolios that have 'convexity' or 'gamma', the latter method gives exact results.

For the business enterprise that falls outside the banking sector, the problem of quantifying risk need not be of such great concern. However, from time to time an involved risk quantification problem may arise. The solution then is to make use of the services of qualified people to do the necessary calculations. It is doubtful that, in the normal course of events, a business would have extremely complex portfolio of risks to manage. The purpose of this book is to make you aware of the fundamental problems that may be involved. That is not to say that you will necessarily or even be likely to have to deal with them.

Hedgeable Risk

All risks are manageable and there is almost a surfeit of techniques available for managing risk. However, from the definition of hedging, it must already be clear that not all risks are hedgeable. In the business of hedging, we are concerned with the technique of assuming risks that offset other risks. This is such a powerful and effective technique that more and more hedging opportunities are created every day. Nevertheless, we must distinguish between those risks that are hedgeable and those that are not.

Risks that are not hedgeable are those for which there are no offsetting risks readily available. The lack of offsetting risk may be temporary, due to the lack of an appropriate instrument, or it may be permanent, due to the nature of the risk itself.

Many of the risks that cannot be hedged are insurable, or at least partly insurable. Some of the common types of risk that fall outside the scope of the business of hedging are credit risk, liquidity risk, legal risk and operational risk.

Distinction between Manageable Risk and Hedgeable Risk

Returning to the example of the shoe merchant, we would be unable to hedge his risk, namely that people may not buy shoes at his chosen location. He can manage that risk only by being careful in his selection of location. In addition, throughout the life of the business he should keep a watch on the changing demography of the area and other business developments. If he fails to be on constant guard, he may be caught unawares by changes that could adversely affect his custom. He could also manage the risk by diversifying, i.e. by opening other stores in different locations, but he cannot actually hedge the risk.

However, the risks that are not hedgeable are also risks that are generally well known. Not every business may be managing these risks as well as it might, but every responsible businessperson is surely aware of credit risk – the risk that his debtors may default. Credit risk is hedgeable to be sure. Credit derivatives are a growing part of the derivatives market. However, our concern is primarily with market risk and how that can be hedged. In one way or another, every business controls operational risk. Liquidity is another problem that every businessperson is very well aware of. In most if not all businesses, a lot of time and effort is spent in addressing this problem.

The real power of the business of hedging lies in the fact that it addresses those risks against which most businesses feel helpless. There are basically three types of risk in this category: the price of money, the price of commodities, and systematic risk. They are all pervasive, but businesses are seldom properly equipped to deal with them. It is estimated that in the US more than 70 per cent of all business failures are directly or indirectly attributable to the adverse influence of one or more of these three risks, which is why they are known as the three risks of the apocalypse.

The Three Risks of the Apocalypse

Although the basic idea of a hedge is the same no matter what the risk involved may be, the hedging instruments, the techniques and specific problems encountered with each type of risk differ. It is also necessary to identify what type of risk a particular business faces at a particular time. One might think that identifying and typifying risk is a straightforward matter, and sometimes it is. Very often, though, it may be difficult to identify even the fact that a particular risk exposure exists. Once the exposure has been identified, you may find that it can be classified under more than one risk. The question that then arises is what the most appropriate hedging technique would be.

Of course, nobody knows a business as well as the people involved in it and nobody knows your business as well as you do. A book such as this therefore cannot carry out the required risk analysis for every business. It is hoped, however, that enough direction can be gained from the analyzes and discussions that follow to enable it to serve as a general guide for most businesses. Let us look at the three apocalyptic risks.

The Price of Money

In financial terms it is trite to say that the rate of interest is the price of money. It is not only trite, it happens to be true. Financial management parameters also suggest that there should be a certain amount of gearing in every business. Without gearing, your business is like a motor vehicle that has only low gear. You may put a lot of torque on to the road, but you will never pick up speed. If you are properly geared, as the principles of financial management suggest, you are subject to interest rate risk.

Of course, some businesses are geared and cash-flush simultaneously. If you are cash-flush, you need to invest it in some way, even if only in the very short term. The moment you have money, you are subject to interest rate risk.

However, there is another aspect to the price of money. The price of money is also what its value is in terms of other currencies. How much will a business have to pay for US dollars if it has Japanese yen? The exchange rate is the price of one currency in terms of another. It is therefore another aspect of the price of money. Many businesses have failed because they have not, or have inadequately, provided for moves in rates of exchange.

In the business of hedging there is a great similarity in the way that both of these rate risks are dealt with. There are strategies that offset adverse interest rate and exchange rate moves in one hedge. This is so because they are both factors of the price of money. Nevertheless, it is necessary to discuss the two factors separately because there are differences in their source and effect. Also, a business does not always face both elements of risk at the same time.

Interest Rates

If you do not heed Shakespeare in your business life, you might be either a lender or a borrower of money. Whichever one of the two, you may well be subject to interest rate risk. If you are a lender, or an investor in interest-bearing assets, you may be at risk if interest rates fall. Conversely, if you are a borrower, your risk might lie in an interest rate hike. Depending on the circumstances, the risk might be in short-term, medium-term or long-term interest rates.

Either if you are at risk because you have invested or because you have borrowed, your exposure to interest rate risk will be direct and probably linear. This means that the interest you pay or receive will be directly affected by a change in rates – if they change, your rate also changes. Your risk will be linear if your rate is linked to another interest rate. This means that for every point that interest rate changes, your linked rate will also change by a point.

In addition, you may be exposed to interest rates by convexity. That is a non-linear exposure which means you run a risk of loss when interest rates change, but it is a risk that is neither necessarily contemporaneous nor linear. Such an exposure might exist in a business that is economically sensitive to interest rates. An example might be a realtor. In a particular market, house sales might drop because of higher interest rates. New mortgages become more expensive and buyers will therefore be less aggressive in the market. If the situation continues, some sellers will be willing to sell at lower prices. Sales will pick up, but earned commissions might still be down since they are based on a lower selling price. In such a case, the realtor has suffered a loss due directly to a rise in interest rates, but to quantify such loss proactively would be difficult.

There are a number of ways to hedge interest rates. The Chicago Board of Trade's (CBOT) US Treasury Futures contract is said to be the most actively traded futures contract in the world. In its publication *Practical Uses of Treasury Futures* 1999, p.1, it states that hedging activity accounts for most futures trading.

Foreign Exchange Risk

Many businesses are exposed to foreign exchange risk, which is associated with a change in the relative value of one currency to another. Consider an import/export firm, situated in the UK, that sells bottled water from Canada to a retail chain in Japan. It has to pay for the water in Canadian dollars from its own resources in British pounds, while the Japanese firm undertakes to pay in US dollars. Granted, the situation might be somewhat unlikely, in that firms will usually try to do a whole transaction in one currency, such as US dollars. However, the postulated situation may well arise, especially if there are arbitrage profits to be had from using multiple currencies. Unless the firm can implement all legs of the transaction simultaneously, it will lose if either the Canadian or the US dollar strengthens against the pound. In fact, both will probably strengthen at the same time if the change is as a result of a weakness in the pound. The firm is in double jeopardy.

Once again, the risk here is direct and linear. However, a business might be exposed to foreign exchange risk without having any foreign exchange position. Consider a US hotelier who is dependent on tourism. He may have acquired quite a bit of goodwill, say among Japanese tourists. If the yen drops in value against the dollar, holidays in the US will become very expensive for Japanese tourists. Fewer people will be able to afford US holidays and our hotelier friend will suffer a greater number of vacant bed-nights. His loss of profit will clearly not be equal to the change in value of the two currencies and the effect of the change will make itself felt only a while after the currency fluctuation. Yet his loss is directly attributable to the change in the exchange rate. His business undoubtedly faces foreign exchange risk.

Foreign exchange markets are probably the most frequently used and best developed in the modern financial world. The hedging instruments appropriate in hedging the risks involved in the price of money will be dealt with in the next chapter. Because of their frequent use and the large number of transactions, you can be sure that these markets are very efficient. They are also very liquid. Once you master the basics of hedging, you will find that protecting your business from currency risk is quite straightforward.

Commodity Price Risk

Most businesses use commodities. Commodities might be the subject matter of the business, as in the case of a scrap metal dealer or an import/export business; they might be the raw materials required for the manufacture of items; or they might be quite incidental to the business, such as the use of diesel fuel by a trucking company.

For whatever reason commodities are dealt in, their value usually plays a substantial role in the risk exposure of a business. If a business purchases raw material such as aluminium for the production of window and doorframes, the price paid for the metal will play an important role in the profit the business makes when it sells the finished product. Say, for instance, that while holding the inventory, or perhaps just after the order for the purchase of the metal has been given, the price drops substantially, some competitors will be purchasing at that lower price. They will therefore be able to sell at a lower price than the business that made the earlier purchase at the higher price.

Consider also another scenario. Our window frame manufacturer is called upon to quote on a big order. He manages to get the order, but his quote is based on today's price of raw material, while the contract requires delivery in six months' time. If the price of aluminium rises, the business may have to manufacture at a loss.

Commodity price risk is usually direct and linear. If the price of the commodity rises or falls, the value of present inventory and the cost of purchasing inventory rises or falls in tandem.

All these commodity risks present hedging opportunities. Hedging the price risk of commodities is in fact the first known use of the technique. The first futures markets were founded for the purpose of dealing with the hedging requirements of the agricultural and mining industries. There are therefore adequate ways and means of dealing with each one and more of the above examples.

Systemic Risk

Stocks in listed companies are said to carry individual stock, or non-systemic risk. According to modern portfolio theory, the risk inherent in common stocks is defined as individual stock risk. By holding equity in a particular company, the investor is at risk of the market's valuation of that particular stock. Non-systemic risk is a combination of industry risk and the risks peculiar to that company.

The factors that create industry risk include the introduction of new technologies, changing growth rates, the costs of production, supply and demand for the industry product, and industry earnings. Company risk is peculiar to a particular company within an industry. It is created by, among other things, the competence of management, its marketing strategies, status in the marketplace, innovation and financial performance.

It is obviously not only investors in publicly listed companies who face such non-systemic risk. Every business is subject to non-systemic risk. Not only do the owners, partners and/or shareholders of every business face this risk, so does every employee of the firm. Every one of them depends on the performance of that business, either for a return on investment or for their livelihood, or both.

Non-systemic risk is actually the fabric of business. It is the risk that every entrepreneur, manager and employee of a business realizes and willingly accepts when he joins the enterprise. They are in the business precisely because they believe that with their talents, knowledge and competence they can face and beat those risks to make a profit.

The insidious risk is systemic risk. This is market risk, created by the volatility of the overall market. Systemic risk is all-pervasive. Its effects will vary from time to time and from sector to sector throughout an economy. The volatility of the overall market, or any sector thereof, is a direct result of the general economic environment, as evidenced by inflation, unemployment, investment and government policy. No business can escape systemic risk.

Fortunately, modern financial instruments allow us to separate systemic risk from non-systemic risk. When the two are separated, systemic risk can be hedged. The business owner is then left to take care of only the non-systemic risk. This is the risk that he must regard himself as totally competent to manage otherwise he would not, or should not be in that business. He will then be free to concentrate on his strengths, building his business without the Damoclean sword of systemic risk hanging over his head.

One might well ask what practical effect systemic risk has on the ordinary, average business. The answer is multi-faceted. Systemic risk manifests itself through price moves in stocks. In other words, if the general economic environment favours companies in the industrial sector, their individual stock prices will rise. If the rise is pretty widespread, the Dow Jones Industrial Average will respond positively (the Dow is the principal indicator of the performance of the shares of companies in the industrial sector quoted on the New York Stock Exchange, and is generally regarded as an indicator of the state of the industrial sector of the US economy at large). If economic factors are not favourable, the opposite will happen.

The manifestation of favourable or unfavourable economic conditions in the US industrial sector will be the move of the Dow. Underlying that manifestation are market and policy factors that either support or inhibit the financial performance of those companies that make up the Dow. Since the effect of those factors must be widespread for the Dow to react to them, every firm in that sector of the economy will be subject to those factors. They may not all be subject to them to the same extent, and probably the effect of the factors will not be the same on every one of them, yet those factors will be there for every business to deal with.

We all know that when the Dow, for example, moves down, not all stocks included in the index go down. Some stock prices actually rise. Not all companies will show less profit, some companies' profits will actually grow. None of this is really the point. Whatever the outcome of any particular company's financial performance, it was achieved under certain systemic conditions. If systemic conditions were different, performance would have been different.

This brings us to the conclusion that the general economic environment, as manifested by the performance of listed companies operating therein, either supports or inhibits the financial performance of every business that operates in that economic environment. This is really a roundabout way of saying something quite axiomatic: the state of the economy affects us all, for better or for worse.

When economic conditions in our industry are not favourable, we will underachieve. Profits will flounder, even disappear. Even if we do well despite conditions, we would have done better under better conditions. If a company can sensibly hedge itself against an adverse change in general economic conditions, its profitability must improve, its share value will be enhanced through its better performance, and it will definitely gain in competitiveness.

The real problem here is correlation. A particular company's financial performance will not necessarily correlate perfectly with any index. The risk is definitely not linear or direct. When the correct hedging technique is used, this need not be such a severe problem. If a truly exact correlation is required, there are candidates available that have the necessary expertise to deal with this. It will always be advantageous to make use of firms with specific skills whenever you are unsure of exactly how effective your hedges will be. As you learn more about the tools and then the techniques of hedging, these obstacles will be less of a problem.

PART TWO

The Tools of
Financial Hedging

The Derivatives

Know Your Tools

In ancient times the Phoenicians and later the Romans navigated mostly by watching the sun and hugging the coastline. It is believed that the Carthaginians even managed to circumnavigate the African continent steering their ships in this fashion. The Arabs contributed their scientific knowledge of the heavens over the next centuries and sea travel became somewhat safer. The Vikings made it to North America via the icy northern route, apparently by means of a combination of coast-hugging, island-hopping, ocean currents and lots of luck.

Nevertheless, the Europeans were pretty much stuck in Europe unless they were willing to face the fearsomely difficult overland route to the East. Travelling overland as they did, they would never even have learned of the Americas, much less reached them. Travelling by sea was a simpler solution to their problems. What they lacked were the proper tools of navigation.

When Prince Henry the Navigator discovered the navigational potential of the magnetic compass, they could at least tell in which direction they were travelling. But the problem of navigation had still not been solved. There remained the question of how much distance had been travelled. With the invention of the sextant, only part of that question was answered. People could now tell how far north or south they had travelled as well as the local time. The most difficult question was yet to be resolved: how far west or east had they gone? That question could only be answered once a reliable chronometer had been invented. A chronometer would keep the time of their home port throughout the journey, so that this time could then continuously be compared with the time readings taken at their present position. The time difference would tell them how far east or west they had travelled from their home port.

Steering your business is much like steering a ship. You have to navigate it properly or you might end up in a place you would rather not be. You cannot navigate properly if you do not have the navigational tools and the knowledge to use them. Your financial compass, sextant and chronometer have already been invented. Some of them are in this chapter, waiting for you to discover them.

The Fundamentals of Derivatives

Derivatives are so called because they derive their values from the values of some other financial instruments or commodities. They are not traded for their own sake but for the sake of what underlies them.

Gold is a commodity that is bought and sold because people want it – or do not want it. An option to buy or to sell gold at a certain price is merely an agreement giving the holder certain rights. Gold underlies the option. The rights given by the option have a value because gold has a value. If gold suddenly lost all commercial value, the options would have no value either. On the other hand, should there suddenly be a great increase in the value of gold because people were desperately trying to acquire the metal, the options would become extremely valuable at the same time.

The option is therefore a derivative. In this example, its value is derived from and dependent upon the value of gold. Gold is the primary instrument and it is referred to as the underlier, or the underlying of the derivative. The market, on which the physical gold trades, is called the underlying market.

The Fear of Derivatives

The term 'derivative' scares many people in business. So many media stories, scandals and high-profile crimes have included this little word, that it seems to be the considered opinion of most business people that it is territory to be shied away from. It is not. People commit crimes with knives, but that does not mean that you don't keep knives in your kitchen, does it?

There is a whole litany of international financial disasters linked to derivatives. Many very large, very old and very important firms have suffered severe losses and failures because of derivatives trading. They lie like shipwrecks dotting the financial coastline. But derivatives did not wreck them – they were all wrecked on the rocks of greed, fear and ignorance, and some very bad seamanship. A bad workman will always blame his tools. Derivatives were merely the tools whereby the financial navigators were supposed to steer the ship, but they made a total hash of it.

We said in the previous chapter that in order to hedge an existing risk we have to go out and take upon ourselves another risk, one that is negatively correlated with the risk that we already have. How can we do that? The most practical way is by means of some appropriate derivative instrument. A derivative instrument is by definition an instrument that involves risk. To hold a position in derivatives is to hold risk – financial risk. Consequently, they are dangerous instruments, to be handled with care. They bear risk because they are designed to do so. They are designed to have risk because they are supposed to have it. They would be useless if they were risk-free.

You cannot mine, build or undertake civil engineering projects without dynamite. It is probably one of the most useful excavating tools to come out of the Industrial Revolution. After its invention, mankind no longer had to use muscle power to break rocks. Severe limitations on extractable ore disappeared with Mr Nobel's little invention. A well-trained person can use dynamite with almost as much accuracy as a doctor uses a scalpel. You can use it to blow away a mountain, or make a tunnel through it, or a hole the size of a pin through a wooden door. But the moment you treat TNT carelessly or you lose your respect for it, it will blow up in your face. In the mining industry, a person is not allowed to use dynamite unless he has acquired what is known as a blasting certificate. Derivatives are financial dynamite. This book is designed to give you a blasting certificate in derivatives – at least insofar as they are used for the purposes of financial hedging.

Flexibility and Categorization

Because derivatives are so useful and flexible, they tend to have endless permutations. People are continuously inventing structures and combinations, creating all sorts of weird and wonderful concoctions. We shall deal with some of these. Derivatives are classified and categorized in so many overlapping ways that the subject can become quite confusing. We are going to keep it basic and simple. It does not need to be confusing. We will stick with the basic categories that aid understanding and try to work from the general to the specific. Once you understand the principles well, the rest will be easy.

There are two categories of derivatives – over-the-counter (OTC) derivatives and exchange-traded derivatives.

Over-The-Counter Derivatives (OTCs)

A financial instrument is called an over-the-counter traded instrument if it can be traded outside a formal exchange. Most OTCs are created by and traded through banks. Large brokerages make the markets in specific issues. Sometimes large corporations and financial institutions also create OTCs. By far the greater number of trades are done over the telephone. Prices are disseminated over services, such as those provided by Reuters and others.

The OTC markets are accessible to any company or private individual. They seldom cater for amounts below $1 million, but certain banks may entertain deals for lower sums. The best way to make use of these instruments is to approach your bank. Most commercial banks will deal with OTC derivatives because their availability enhances the service offered to the client. Through offering derivatives, banks allow an additional dimension of risk management to their client. It also gives the banks room to manoeuvre.

Every bank's credit department evaluates the credit risk of a client. Thus, they establish a credit line that reflects the maximum exposure they are prepared to have to a particular client at any given time. Consider the case where the client has already made full use of all the credit on his credit line. In that case, the bank cannot really transact any further business with him. For example, the client may have a need to hedge against adverse changes in interest rates to which the use of his credit facilities has exposed him. The bank may not allow him to make an interest rate swap, but it may sell him an interest rate option – assuming the client is willing and able to pay the premium.

The client will now be a better credit risk for the bank. His interest rate position is hedged and he even has some profit potential. Once the bank has received the premium, the bank runs no additional risk.

This example illustrates the situation in principle and many permutations are possible. It is incumbent on both banks and customers to be aware of these possibilities in order to make use of the potential that is already there in the market. Therefore, if your bank does not deal in OTCs on behalf of and with their clients, find one that does.

Forwards and FRAs

Derivative instruments are not all suited to hedging. You will find derivative instruments in the marketplace that are not discussed here. The most common one that deserves to be mentioned is 'forwards'. These are derivatives because they have underlying instruments or commodities from which their values are derived. It is really an agreement to buy and deliver something in the future at a price that is decided now. In the interest rate market, such agreements are known as forward rate agreements (FRAs). It is an agreement to lend and to borrow money at a specified date in the future, for a specified period at a specified interest rate. The interest rate agreed upon is called the forward rate.

The forward rate or forward price is not the same as the spot price, because the forward price is a price projected into the future. The forward price is not the same thing as the futures price. The futures price is the price of futures contracts on the futures exchanges. There may be a close correlation between the forward price of a thing and its futures price, but in principle they are entirely different.

Forwards are used to contract out of risk. The price or rate of a future transaction is fixed now. Once the price is fixed, there is no more price risk as far as that transaction is concerned. It is therefore an effective way of avoiding risk. However, as we know from the definition of hedging, avoiding risk is not the same thing as hedging risk. We shall deal only with those derivative instruments that are suited to the purposes of hedging.

Swaps

The OTC derivative that is most often used is the swap. It is generally available, especially in the interest rate and currency markets, and is, also widely used in certain commodity markets, such as oil and gas. Swaps are very often standardized by banks and they will have certain standard instruments available that are designed for frequent use. Nevertheless, swaps can be tailor-made to the requirements of parties. Swaps are never traded on an exchange and are thus only OTC instruments.

Options

Options are derivative instruments, as has already been mentioned. They are available as OTCs and as exchange traded instruments. The market on which the underlying is traded determines whether the options thereon are exchange traded or OTC traded. If the underlying is not traded on an exchange, the option will not be traded on an exchange.

Options are available on every kind of underlier, from interest rates and currencies to commodities and equities. OTC options are available through banks and finance houses as well as through certain large corporations, such as major oil companies.

Exchange-Traded Derivatives

Only two types of derivatives are actually traded on exchanges – options and commodity futures contracts. All futures contracts are referred to as commodity futures, but the instruments that underlie them are not necessarily 'commodities' in the ordinary sense of the word. The term 'commodity' has developed over many years in the financial markets. Today the most acceptable definition is anything that is or can be the subject matter of a futures contract. What limitations that places on the meaning of the term will be discussed when we deal with commodity futures contracts.

Commodity Exchanges

The exchanges themselves are usually non-profit associations of their members. The exchanges do not buy, sell or in any way deal in the products that trade on them. Their sole function is to provide the necessary facilities to their members to conduct trading. Only members of an exchange are allowed to trade on that exchange. It is for this reason that any party wishing to conduct business on an exchange and who is not a member of that exchange must do so through a member. Some brokers are members of an exchange and can act on your behalf directly. Other brokers work through members who have undertaken to conduct trading on behalf of the brokers and their clients. When you decide to embark on trading derivatives on an exchange, you must appoint a broker or deal with a member firm directly. There should be a high degree of mutual trust between a broker and his client. Spend time on selecting your broker or broking member. You must be happy that you are comfortable working with that person or firm.

An exchange is nothing more or less than a physical marketplace where buyers come to buy and sell certain products. For example, fresh produce markets are specifically structured and organized to facilitate the buying and selling of fresh produce at a particular location for onward distribution. It is intended to be a place where producers and users of the product can get together and openly discover prices.

Some Functions of Commodity Exchanges

Price discovery is the major function of an exchange. It is a large auction mart where producers come to offer goods or products and users bid against each other to obtain them. Such an open and transparent process is the fairest means yet devised to discover the proper market price or commercial value of a particular thing on a particular day at a particular place. These auction marts create a focal point for trading and thus oil the wheels of commerce. The prices at which transactions are done on an exchange establish the value of the commodities traded. The exchange disseminates all the trading information, which is extremely valuable for increasing the effectiveness of the marketplace and without which the modern free market would be unable to function.

Exchanges started as open-outcry exchanges, but technological advances have overtaken them. Today many exchanges are totally electronic. They have become 'virtual' exchanges. The original open outcry exchanges still operate in that way, but they have all adopted electronic trading systems for after-hours and overnight trading.

It is also the function of the exchange to discipline its members. It is responsible for ensuring that members conduct their business on the exchange in a fair and equitable manner. The governing committee of an exchange therefore establishes the rules that govern the conduct of its members. If you ever have reason to complain of the behaviour of an exchange member, the exchange is the right place to lodge your complaint. The committee will investigate it and assess the appropriate penalty, if any. The exchanges will usually be prepared to arbitrate disputes between members and customers if they are requested to do so.

Commodity Futures Contracts

Futures contracts are derivatives that trade on commodity futures exchanges specifically brought into existence for the sole purpose of trading them. Futures contracts have commodities, equity indices, oil, natural gas and innumerable other standardized products as their underliers. Commodity futures exchanges trade only futures contracts and options on these. They are created specifically to trade the futures contracts and not the underlying commodities. Although provision is made for delivery and acceptance of the underlying in terms of futures contracts, this is not the idea behind a futures exchange. It is not a market intended for the trading of the underlying commodity. Spot markets are designed for that purpose.

Commodity Options

By contrast, commodity options are generally available on exchanges that are primarily intended to deal in instruments that underlie the option. To put it differently, when an exchange is set up to deal in a specific type of instrument or commodity, it will often also offer options on that instrument or commodity. The London Metal Exchange (LME), for example, is an exchange dealing in spot metals. In other words, it deals in the buying and selling of the physical metals for 'spot', meaning buying and selling of the metals for immediate delivery. It also offers options to purchase or sell metals at a future date. The metals are the primary instruments and the options are their derivatives.

In addition, specialist option exchanges have come into existence. The Chicago Options Exchange is the largest options exchange in the world. It offers options on equities and equity indices. In this case, the equities and indices underlie the options.

Finally, commodity futures exchanges also offer options on futures contracts. Keep in mind, though, that exchanges do not necessarily offer options on all futures contracts that are traded on the exchange. The difference between a commodity option on a commodity and an option on a commodity future is that should the buyer of an option on a futures contract exercise his option, he will be either long or short a futures contract, not the commodity underlying the futures. Against that, when the holder of a commodity option exercises the option, he will either receive or sell the actual commodity, depending on the type of option he held.

In order to illustrate this difference, consider a plumbing firm that purchases a call option to hedge the price of copper. If the option is purchased on the LME, the underlying is a certain quantity of copper. If the option is exercised, the firm will have to pay for and take delivery of that quantity of physical copper. It could, of course, put the copper back on the market to realize a profit, although that might not be what it had in mind when the option was bought. By contrast, had it purchased a copper futures option on the New York Mercantile Exchange (Nymex), it would have had a different result. If the option had moved into the money and the firm had then exercised it, it would have received a long position in copper futures. It could then dispose of the futures contract to realize a profit.

An option on a futures contract is thus a derivative of a derivative. The futures contract trades in a market where its value is determined by market forces. Market forces that drive futures contract prices are based on the underlying market. Therefore, an option on a futures contract is actually a further step away because it trades with its prices based on the price of the underlying futures contracts and not on the prices of the underlying of the futures contracts.

CHAPTER FOUR

Financial Swaps

Background

As the name suggests, a swap is a two-way arrangement between parties. It is in the first instance an agreement, a binding contract between two parties to exchange one thing for another. An exchange necessarily implies that each party to the exchange will give something and each party will receive something. But a financial swap is not the traditional exchange of goods that one might expect to find in pre-monetary societies. It is not the 'I shall exchange my five oxen for your 50 goats' type of situation. This latter transaction is the traditional agreement of barter or exchange. The element that is different in a financial swap is not the basic structure of the agreement but the subject matter of the exchange.

The Subject Matter of a Financial Swap

In a financial swap, two income streams are exchanged. One flow of money is exchanged for another. By the terms 'income stream' and 'flow of money' we merely mean that a series of payments of money over a period of time is involved. For example, person P undertakes to make ten equal payments to company C. Ignore for the moment what the reason for the undertaking may be. She undertakes to make one payment at the end of every six months, for the next five years. That undertaking represents an income stream for C. It can also be described as a flow of money from P to C. This arrangement is shown in Figure 4.1, in which the arrow illustrates a cash flow from P to C. The period of the cash flow is represented by the length of the arrow and the number of payments by the stars on the arrow.

The traditional barter agreement has the object of achieving an exchange of goods of equal value. In our example of the traditional barter exchange above, the parties would agree to that deal only if, in their system of values, one ox were equal in value to five goats. However, in the modern financial swap, we are not trying to arrange an exchange for equal value. We are trying to arrange for an exchange of unequal value.

Figure 4.1

A flow of money

That sounds daft, doesn't it? The question at the back of every-one's mind must be: 'Why would anyone exchange something of value for something of lesser value?' Putting the question in that way is not correct either.

Differentiated Returns on Principal

Let us consider the situation. We are trying to create a risk. A risk must involve the possibility of gain as well as loss. Since we are exchanging a stream of payments of money and not goods, there would be no sense in exchanging an amount of money for an equal amount of money. The only possible risk would be default by one party in making one or more of the payments. That involves a risk only of loss, but none of gain. So, if the exchanged income streams were equal in value and remained equal throughout the period, the exercise would be pointless.

What if the exchanged money flows were not necessarily of the same value but were based on the same value (the principal) yet reflected fluctuating returns determined by market conditions? To investigate this question, we will flesh out our example. Person P is actually Paula McDermott, a lady who owns a rather large cosmet-ics firm that manufactures and markets a whole range of cosmetics under her own brand name. She was introduced to company C through her bank. Company C is Champignon Trust, an investment trust, with a brimful of money to invest. We will come to all the whys and wherefores later. For now, we will concentrate on how the deal is structured.

The Basic Structure of Swaps

Paula borrowed a large sum of money from Champignon Trust for a period of five years. In terms of the agreement, however, she promptly and immediately put that amount of money on deposit with the trust for a period of five years. Her deposit serves as collat-eral for the loan. At the end of the five years the deposit matures, Champignon Trust grabs the principal and Paula's debt is extin-guished (see the loan and deposit arrows in Figure 4.2.).

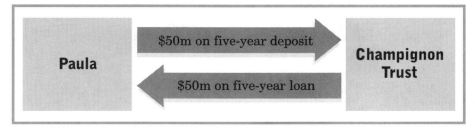

The basic arrangement of the principal in a swap

However, if the interest rate that Paula were charged on the loan were to be the same as the interest rate she is paid on the deposit, her net receipts would be zero. Champignon Trust's net receipts would also be zero. So there is exactly zero chance that they will enter into such an arrangement.

The arrangement can be meaningful only if there is risk. This means that at least one of the interest rates must not be a fixed rate but must be a variable or floating rate. Assume the transaction starts out on the basis that both interest rates are of the same value, but that the rate Paula pays for the loan will be fixed for the period of the arrangement. The interest rate that Champignon pays on the deposit will be the six-month Libor (London Inter Bank Offered Rate) rate. The total cash flow arrangement is illustrated in Figure 4.3. How we obtain two rates of interest that are of the same value at the start will be dealt with presently.

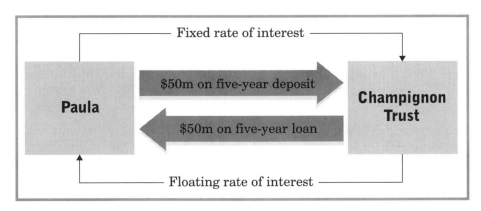

The cash flow arrangement of a coupon swap

The cash flow arrangement in the example is referred to as a fixed against floating swap. It has various aliases, including a coupon swap and a vanilla swap.

The Notional Principal

This example illustrates another basic element of a swap, namely that the principal, upon which the cash flows are based, never actually changes hands. The loan and deposit are really legal fictions. For that reason, the principal is usually referred to as the notional principal.

Cash flow Periodicity

The frequency of payments can be any agreed frequency. As hedgers, we will select the payment frequency to suit the risk we intend to hedge. Although it is usual, it is not a necessary requirement for the payments in each leg to be at identical intervals. And even if they are, they are not required to be contemporaneous.

Such non-coincidence of payments is unusual and gives rise to other complex and subtle risks. The hedger would be well advised to steer away from them. Quarterly, semi-annual and annual payments are all usual.

Netting of Payments

When payments are contemporaneous, netting of payments is usual and advisable. This merely means that party A does not make full payment of his interest instalment against full payment by party B. The interest payments that are due are subtracted from one another. Only the party that pays the higher amount at that stage pays the net amount by which his payment exceeds the payment due from the other party. This is the most satisfactory way of implementation. It also reduces credit risk to the net amount rather than to the full instalment. Unfortunately, the legal enforceability of netting agreements is under doubt in some European countries.

Fixing the Interest Rates for Swaps

It has already been mentioned that the interest rates upon which the cash flows are based can be at any rate. Yet in practice, the six-month Libor is most often used as the variable in coupon swaps. Nevertheless, that is a mere statistic. The important fact to note is that the maturity of Libor used will be the same as the time between payments in the swap. In other words, if the swap payments are made quarterly, three-month Libor will be appropriate, while if annual payments are required, 12-month Libor will be the applicable rate.

Interest rates are agreed upon and fixed at the beginning of the swap, as is to be expected. The floating interest rate is fixed in the beginning by reference to the agreed upon variable. Thus, a quarterly instalment will initially be fixed at the start of the period, but will be paid only in three months' time. Interest is fixed in advance and paid in arrears. When that first instalment is paid, the rate for the second instalment will be fixed, again by reference to the agreed-upon variable. Each party knows in advance at the beginning of each period, what its payment will be at the end of that period.

The principle of this methodology is illustrated in Figure 4.4, in which the movements of the actual interest rate index are related to the fixing points of the floating leg and the paying points for both legs in a coupon swap the mechanism has important implications for the pricing of swaps and the determination of the swap rate.

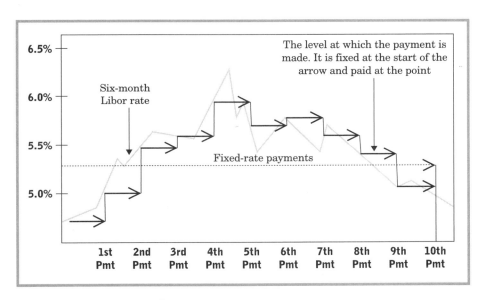

Figure 4.4

Fixing the interest rates for swaps

The Swap Rate

The swap would be most effective if the starting interest rates for the two income streams were identical. In order for them to be the same, the present value of each income stream has to be equal to the present value of the other. The present value of the fixed income stream is quite easy to calculate because once it is fixed, the total cash flow for the whole period will be known.

The floating income stream is the problematic one. The floating income stream in this case is six-month Libor. That rate is known and fixed at the start. The amount that the payer of the floating rate will pay in six months' time is therefore known on day one. However, since it is unknown what the six-month Libor will be in six months' time, we do not know what amount of interest the payer of the floating rate will pay at the end of 12 months.

The whole idea of entering a swap arrangement to hedge is to establish what is known as a par swap. A par swap is a swap that has no value for either party. Imagine a swap with a fixed interest rate leg that is extremely high in relation to the floating rate leg. This arrangement would have a very high value for the person receiving the fixed rate. Alternatively, consider the situation if the fixed interest rate leg were extremely low. Then the swap would have a very high value for the person paying the low, fixed interest rate while receiving a much greater cash flow from the floating interest rate leg. Somewhere in between these two extremes is a fixed-rate payment at some median that favours neither party.

Obviously, the problem of par is solved by a careful choice of the fixed rate. The trouble comes in determining what this median rate is. How do we get the parties to agree that the deal has no value for either of them? The rocket scientists have a way of calculating these things. Fortunately, however, we do not have to break our heads over this problem. The market for swaps is so great and so liquid at so many maturities that every need can be catered for. The fixed interest rate leg of a swap is determined by the market. You will find the rates of interest for the fixed interest rate leg of a swap quoted in the financial press. They are quoted at various maturities and are referred to as the swap rate.

The Risk in Interest Rate Swaps

For us as hedgers, the most important element is to ask what the risk is that we assume by using a particular instrument. I refer of course to the risk that we assume voluntarily, not to any subtle or hidden risks. In a later section, I shall deal with the other risks that are involved in different derivatives. At this stage, we must look at the direct voluntary risk, the risk we want to assume in order to hedge. This situation can be illustrated in the context of our previous example (*see* Table 4.1).

Paula, who is paying the fixed rate, will be at risk that the variable rate may float lower and cause her to pay in more. However, she will profit when interest rates rise. Champignon Trust, being the payer of the floating rate, faces the risk that the Libor-linked rate will float higher, in which case it will have to pay in more and the transaction will become more expensive.

Generalizing from this example, we can say that the payer of the fixed leg will risk a fall in rates, while the payer of the floating leg will risk a rise in rates.

Party	Pays	Receives	Net risk
Paula	Fixed interest rate	Floating interest rate	Interest rates will fall
Champignon Trust	Floating interest rate	Fixed interest rate	Interest rates will rise

Table
4.1

The risk assumed by the parties in our example

Types of Interest Rate Swaps

The most confusing thing about interest rate swaps is the different names and terminologies used. One tends to think that a change in name means that the thing itself must be different. Whichever name you hear in the marketplace, keep the basic swap of income streams in mind. By whatever name the arrangement is called, that is still what is happening. Let us get into some name-calling to see what sense we can make of it.

Coupon Swap

Because the cash flows in the swap between Paula and Champignon Trust are based on interest rates, it is known as an interest rate swap. Because it is a fixed against floating rate swap, it is called a coupon swap. Such uncomplicated swaps are also known as vanilla swaps. This is the most common type of interest rate swap. The swap in the example has a maturity date in more than two years. It is therefore also referred to as a term swap. If it were for a period of no more than two years, it would be termed a money market swap.

Basis Swap

It is possible, of course, to swap two streams of income, based on all sorts of things. Both streams may be based on floating rates, as long as they are not based on the same rate. One floating rate in the swap could be based on six-month Libor, while the other could be based on three-month Libor. One of the rates could even be based on the prime lending rate of some specified bank. Such a floating against floating interest rate swap is called a basis swap because the spread between the two rates is known as the basis.

Consider, for example, a swap where the one cash flow is based on six-month Libor and the other on three-month Libor. Assume that at the start of the swap, the six-month Libor is 6 per cent and the three-month rate is 6.25 per cent. The basis can be calculated either as the difference between the six-month and the three-month rate, or vice versa. It does not matter, as long as one is consistent. Using the first option in our example, we would say the basis is −25 points (6 per cent − 6.25 per cent). This means that the basis is weak, viewed from this perspective.

The basis can weaken even further (become more negative) or strengthen (become more positive) due to the relative movement of the two rates. The risk to each party depends on changes in the basis rather than on changes in any interest rate. A weakening of the basis in the example will mean that the three-month rate moves higher relative to the six-month rate. The payer of the lower, six-month rate will benefit. Conversely, should the basis strengthen, the payer of the three-month rate will benefit. If we had viewed the basis from the other perspective, i.e. the three-month rate to the six-month-rate, we would get the opposite result. The basis is now +25 points. Should the basis strengthen further, the payer of the six-month rate will benefit. If the basis weakens (becomes less positive), the payer of the three-month rate will benefit.

There is one other way of looking at basis. If the two prices constituting the basis move away from each other, we say the basis widens. If the prices move closer to each other, the basis narrows. From this perspective, it is easy to see that the payer of the higher rate is at risk of a widening of the basis and will benefit from a narrowing. The opposite applies to the payer of the lower rate.

Asset Swap

Even the source of the funding of one of the cash flow streams causes a change of name. If one stream is funded by interest received on an asset owned by one party, the transaction is referred to as an asset swap. This may sound like something other than two income streams being swapped, but it is not. It can only be done with an asset that generates interest rate income, such as a mortgage or government bond.

Therefore, notwithstanding it being an asset swap, the transaction could still be either a vanilla swap or a basis swap. It could be a basis swap only if the interest income received from the asset was a floating interest rate. Moreover, it must always be either a money market or a term swap.

Once again, our major concern is with the risk that is created. It is necessary just to summarize the risk that each party assumes as the swap structures change from type to type. The summary of each party's risk is illustrated in Table 4.2. Cash flows are all based on a notional principal.

Swap type	Cash flow		Risk		Maturity	
	Party A pays	Party B pays	Party A	Party B	2 yrs–	2 yrs +
Coupon/ vanilla	Fixed rate	Floating rate	Rate drop	Rate rise		
	Floating rate	Fixed rate	Rate rise	Rate drop		
Basis swap	Floating rate A	Floating rate B	Rise in A relative to B	Rise in B relative to A		
Asset swap	Income from fixed interest rate bearing asset	Floating rate	Floating rate drops	Floating rate rises	Money market swap	Term swap
	Income 'A' from floating interest-bearing asset	Floating rate B	Rise in rate A relative to rate B	Rise in rate B relative to rate A		

Table 4.2

The parties' assumed risk against different cash flows

Basic Currency Swaps

A further type of swap is currency swaps. Again, the change in name does not really reflect a change in substance. However, there are a number of other changes that are material.

There are professionals who do not regard currency swaps as derivatives, because of the technical definition of a derivative. This technicality need not detain us, because the similarities between a currency swap and an interest rate swap is so overwhelming that the latter is really only a special case of the former.

Income Streams in Currency Swaps

There is no change to the major element common to all swaps namely that two streams of income are exchanged. Both income streams are based on interest rates. The first difference, though, is that each stream of income is denominated in a different currency. If the income streams are denominated in two currencies and both are calculated on a rate of interest, how is the principal denominated?

Principal in a Currency Swap

The principal must be denominated in the same two currencies as the income streams. Consider that in the usual interest rate swap, both cash flows are based on a single principal amount. The amount of principal must provide a value base for the rest to make sense. Thus, when the principal is denominated in two currencies, the principal denominated in the one currency must be equal in value to the principal denominated in the other currency. This, in turn, presupposes that a rate of exchange between the two currencies must have been agreed between the parties, otherwise a parity of value for the principal would not be achieved.

Whereas in an interest rate swap the principal is notional, inasmuch as it never changes hands, in a currency swap the principal denominated in one currency is exchanged for the principal denominated in the other currency. The exchange of principal is required only at maturation. Sometimes the parties agree to an exchange of principal at the outset and it is then referred to as a cash swap.

Establishing a Basic Currency Swap

The basic steps in setting up a currency swap are set out in Table 4.3, from the point of view of the initiating party. Let us analyze the transaction. Because the parties agree to the exchange rate for the principal at the outset, they are no longer at risk of fluctuations in the rate as far as the principal is concerned. They have contracted out of risk. Unlike in an interest rate swap, in a currency swap it is not necessary to have at least one of the cash flows based on a floating interest rate. Both cash flows can therefore be based on the same rate of interest, which leads to the question: where does the risk come from?

Structure of a Basic Currency Swap

It is true that everything starts out at equal value and there is no exchange rate risk as far as the principal is concerned. However, the risk lies in the fluctuations of the exchange rate during the term of the swap. Take the example of my friend Dave. He imports items of hardware from the Far East. The items are small, such as nails, screws, washers and so on, but the quantities are great. He repackages these items in the US and retails them through his chain of franchized outlets.

Dave had occasion to enter into a currency swap with a Japanese bank, brokered through his own bank. The swap involved dollars for yen. The exchange rate of the principal sum of $25 million was agreed at $1= ¥118.82 and the interest rate for the cash flows at 6.75 per cent annually. Interest payments would be made quarterly, fixed

Decide which currencies will be used
Decide what the amount of principal in the 'home' currency is
Agree with a counter party on the exchange rate for the principal of the swap, usually the current spot rate
Agree with the counter party what the period to maturation will be
Agree on the interest rate on which the cash flows will be based
Agree on the timing of the payments

Table 4.3

The basic steps in establishing a standard currency swap

in advance, paid in arrears. Both parties' payments were due on the same day. Maturation was after 24 months. Figure 4.5 illustrates the elements and structure of the deal.

At maturity the yen had appreciated against the dollar and stood at $1= ¥110.902. If Dave had had to repay the principal at the latter rate, it would have cost him $26,785,000 instead of the agreed $25 million which he actually paid. The swap thus prevented a loss to him of $1,785,000 on the principal. The Japanese bank, on the other hand, had to forgo a profit of the same amount. The compensation to both parties was that, at least as far as the principal was concerned, they were not at risk. That is what both of them had wanted to achieve in the first place.

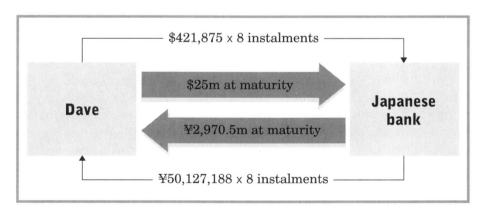

Figure 4.5

Dave's currency swap with a Japanese bank

Risk in a Basic Currency Swap

The risk that each party wished to assume was concerned with the changing value of the instalments. Because of the initial fixing of identical interest rates, Dave knew that he was going to pay a total of $3,375,000 in interest over the period. He also knew that he was going to receive a total of ¥401,017,504 in return. At the agreed exchange rate, the two streams of income would be equal in value.

Dave's risk was that the dollar would appreciate against the yen. If that happened, he would be paying out more and more value in dollars than he was receiving in yen. At the outset, Dave would be able to finance his dollar instalment simply by converting his Japanese yen receipts into dollars. But if the yen depreciated against the dollar, every yen would purchase fewer dollars than before. Dave would thus not have sufficient dollars to pay his dollar instalment after the conversion – he would have to pay in dollars from his own resources.

The Japanese bank, on the other hand, faced the same risk but in an opposite direction. It also knew exactly how much it would receive in dollars and how much yen it would have to disburse against the receipt. Its risk, however, was that the dollar would depreciate against the yen or, conversely, that the yen would appreciate against the US dollar. If that happened, every dollar it received would purchase fewer yen. The bank's receipts in dollars would not be adequate to finance its payments in yen.

As it happened, the yen first deteriorated against the dollar, then appreciated quite substantially. So over the course of the arrangement there were a few times that Dave had to pay in. At those times, the bank gained since it was receiving more value in dollars than it was disbursing in yen.

At the end, though, Dave started making bigger and bigger profits from converting his yen to dollars and then paying his dollar instalment. Every yen he received was buying more dollars than before. His dollar income from converting yen to dollar was continuously giving him more dollars than he required for his payment.

Contrary to Dave's profits, the bank was making losses on the swap. The dollars it was receiving were buying fewer and fewer yen. It had to find yen from other resources in order to finance its instalments to Dave.

Cross-Currency Coupon Swap

The basic currency swap that we have discussed is the only form that is properly called a currency swap. We have seen that the purpose of such a proper currency swap is to create currency risk. However, an interest rate swap and a currency swap are not different in principle. Therefore, a swap can be engineered to create currency risk and interest rate risk at the same time. The only amendment to the currency swap structure discussed above would be that at least one of the cash flows would be linked to a floating interest rate, i.e. apart from being denominated in different currencies, one cash flow would be calculated at a fixed interest rate while the other would be linked to a floating rate.

The fixed to floating rate set-up gives rise to the word 'coupon' in the terminology, while the word 'cross' refers to the fact that it is a cross between a currency and an interest rate swap. Let us consider for a moment what Dave's situation would have been had he gone for such a transaction instead of a straightforward currency swap. Table 4.4 illustrates the risk assumed by each party.

Assume firstly that the dollar instalments he had to pay were linked to the three-month US dollar Libor. All other elements remain the same. Dave would still face the same currency risk as above, namely that the dollar appreciates against the yen. In addition, he would be at risk to a rise in the three-month Libor. The double rate exposure places him in double jeopardy, and demonstrates that swaps are intrinsically linked to the price of money – be it the price in terms of interest or the price in terms of other currencies, or both.

The Cross-Currency Basis Swap

From the terminology, it is already clear what this means. The word 'cross' again indicates that there is interest risk as well currency risk involved and the use of the term 'basis' indicates our old friend, the basis swap. In the basis swap, both cash flows are linked to floating rates – each to a different floating rate. The same linking applies here.

When we discussed the standard currency swap, we said that both cash flows are calculated on a fixed interest rate. If one were to use a floating interest rate index and then link both cash flows to that index, it would just be a standard currency swap. There would be no interest rate risk.

In order to establish a proper cross-currency basis swap, each cash flow has to be linked to a different interest rate index. The currency risk will be the same as in a standard currency swap and the interest rate risk will be the same as in a basis swap. See Table 4.4, which shows these differences systematically.

Complex Currency Swap Types

The clever and innovative people who make the financial world their profession have constructed various weird and wonderful swap concoctions. It is unnecessary for us to go into too much detail with them as it is really the banks' and their traders' business to know these structures intimately. But we do need to know about some of those you are more likely to encounter.

Table 4.4

Swap type	Currencies		Interest		Risk	
	Party A pays	Party B pays	Party A pays	Party B pays	Party A	Party B
Currency swap	Currency A	Currency B	Fixed rate A	Fixed rate A	Currency: A rises against B	Currency: B rises against A
Cross-currency coupon swap	Currency A	Currency B	Fixed rate A	Floating rate B	Currency: A rises against B/interest rate: B drops	Currency: B rises against A/interest rate: B rises
			Floating rate A	Fixed rate B	Currency: A rises against B/interest rate: A rises	Currency: B rises against A/interest rate: A drops
Cross-currency basis swap	Currency A	Currency B	Floating rate A	Floating rate B	Currency: A rises against B/interest rate: A rises against B	Currency: B rises aganst A/interest rate: B rises against A

Currency and cross-currency swaps

The reason we are skimming over them is that they do not really alter the main types discussed above. These swaps have all been put together in complex ways to overcome international and other obstacles that may stand in the way of achieving one of the above types of swaps directly. There is, for example, the circus swap. Contrary to expectations, it does not involve P. T. Barnum as a counter party. It really consists of a number of swaps, sharing one intermediate party with multiple counter parties. The purpose of such a structure is to achieve, in the net result, either a currency swap or a cross-currency basis swap. It may be necessary to take such a circuitous route because, for some reason or another, you may not be able to achieve the desired result directly.

A Circus Swap

Consider the following example. A software-developing firm situated in Los Angeles enters into a dollar coupon swap with a counter party who does business from its New York office. At the same time, the Los Angeles firm's bank arranges a cross-currency, dollar, three-month Libor-linked/deutschmark fixed-rate coupon swap with a bank situated in Bonn. The dollar principal in the cross currency swap is equal to the notional principal in the coupon swap and the time to maturity is the same. The net risk result is the same as if the software-developing firm had done a simple dollar/deutschmark currency swap.

A possible reason for this transaction could be that there was no liquidity for such a straight currency swap at the time the California-based firm required it.

The Cocktail Swap

Another interesting example of the inventiveness of professional traders, is the cocktail swap. This structure can become extremely complex but always involves a single intermediate party. The counter parties will number at least three, but this element is open-ended. Swaps between certain currencies may be very illiquid. This means that it may be extremely difficult and sometimes impossible to find a willing counter party when you need one. The way round this problem is then not to swap the two currencies directly but to use an intermediate currency, such as the dollar. You can understand that if you had to arrange a swap between the South African rand and the Brazilian real, things might become problematic. It is probably easier to swap each for dollars with a dollar interest rate swap thrown in. Depending upon exactly what risks you intended to create, more swap transactions might be required. Whatever the final convoluted structure might be, the result would be a rand/real currency or cross-currency swap.

Commodity Swaps

As the terminology indicates, these swaps have some commodity or other as their underlier. Because it is a swap, it could theoretically have any type of commodity as underlier that the parties may agree. There is only one condition. The swap will not involve swapping one commodity for another, it does not become an exchange or barter. It is still the same creature we have been discussing all along. A swap will involve the swapping of two cash flows. The cash flows will be based on a commodity.

One can be forgiven for arguing that a commodity is a commodity and not a cash flow. What possible application could this have in the real world? In fact, it is a very useful way of constructing a swap if it is done correctly. Keep in mind that the principles of swaps that we have discussed remain the same.

The use of commodity swaps is widespread in the energy and equity markets, but there is no reason in principle why they could not be linked to any standardized commodity. The major oil companies tend to be big players in the energy market.

The commodity swap is achieved through the exchange of cash flows that are based on an agreed index price for that commodity. The index price serves the same purpose here as the interest rate index (e.g. three-month Libor) or exchange rate serves in other swaps. Because we are dealing with cash flows over an agreed period, it follows that the index must be referred to at regular intervals over that period. The underlier of the swap will be a notional amount, linked to a certain quantity of that commodity. It is not the intention of the parties to have the commodity delivered at any stage.

From this discussion, we can see that this type of swap would more properly be called an index swap. In fact, if one considers the very essence of swaps, it would be true to say that all swaps are really index swaps.

To illustrate how a commodity swap might be structured, let us take the example of Triumph Heavy Transport (THT). It runs a fleet of 450 20-wheeler rigs and its greatest single overhead is the price of diesel fuel. In order to protect itself from rising fuel prices, it decides to set up a commodity swap with its major fuel supplier, BP.

A number of oil indexes can be used. *Platt's* is a daily journal reporting oil prices under different categories, or futures price, with an upward or downward adjustment. The parties agree to use the *Platt's* Brent Blend Crude index, since it tracks THT's fuel costs the closest. They also agree that the swap will mature in 12 months.

What in effect happens now is that BP sells to THT an agreed quantity of oil, to be delivered in 12 months' time. The price of the transaction is fixed at that day's price for Brent Blend crude, as indicated by *Platt's* daily journal. THT must therefore pay the fixed price. At the same time, the parties agree that THT sells to BP the same quantity of oil, also to be delivered in 12 months' time. BP will pay the prevailing price for the oil at the date of delivery. BP will therefore pay the floating price. If oil prices rise, it may end up paying more for the oil it buys than it receives for the oil it sells.

If the parties left the deal at that, there would be no income streams. There would be only a single payment at the end of 12 months. If oil prices had fallen, THT will make a net payment. THT's risk on the swap is therefore that oil prices will drop. Obviously, no oil will change hands.

The Cash Flows in a Commodity Swap

In order to create cash flows, the parties now further agree that the price differences will be settled and averaged every three months. They could have made it monthly, or any other period they preferred. This means that at the end of every three months, the price of the oil will be averaged according to the daily reports in *Platt's* journal. That average will then be compared to the fixed rate that THT pays. If the average price is lower than THT's fixed price, THT will pay the difference within five business days. If the average price is higher than the fixed price, BP will pay the difference to THT within five business days. Clearly, the principal amount is never paid. The payments are only for the price differential.

It will be clear from this example, that in principle, this is just another swap using a different index. It will also be plain that the same swap can be done with any commodity, on condition that there is a readily available index.

Equity Index Swaps

An equity swap is really the same thing as a commodity swap. It is just a commodity swap based on an equity index. It is thus quite easily done. The equity index swap will be structured in exactly the same way as the oil example. Two parties will agree on which equity index they wish to base the swap. Assume for the moment that they decide to use the S&P 500 equities index.

The essence of the transaction is as follows. Party A will purchase the basket of shares that make up the index from party B. Delivery of the shares will be made after an agreed period. Party B agrees to purchase the same basket of shares from party A, to be delivered to him on the same day that he delivers his basket of shares to Party A. No shares ever change hands, but this arrangement establishes the notional principal.

The difference in the undertakings will be that party A might agree to pay the price as indicated by the S&P 500 index at the date of the agreement, while party B undertakes to pay the price as indicated by the index on the day of delivery. They then agree to compensate each other for price changes on a regular basis over the period of the agreement.

This arrangement results in party A risking a fall in the index, while party B risks a rise.

Master Agreements and the ISDA

The International Swaps and Derivatives Association Inc., (ISDA) is the principal trade organization of the derivatives industry. It develops and publishes master agreements for swaps and other OTC derivatives which serve as the industry standard documentation.

In 1985 it published a 'Code of Standard Wording, Assumptions and Provisions for Swaps'. This document is known as the ISDA

Swaps Code. It serves as a menu from which clauses containing certain terms and conditions can be drawn on by parties drafting swap agreements. You are well advised to make use of these tried and trusted agreements or to draft your own by drawing on their precedents, rather than trying to reinvent the wheel when structuring a swap. Your bank or broker should really be looking after this matter, but it does not relieve you of the responsibility to check that the documentation is done properly.

Prior to the ISDA, the British Bankers' Association (BBA) drafted some 'Recommended Terms and Conditions for London Interbank Interest Rate Swaps' (BBAIRS). This documentation has largely been superseded by the standard agreements drafted by the ISDA. However, the BBA still plays a significant role in the swap market. Included in its recommended BBAIRS terms was the mechanism for fixing Libor. The BBA also arranged with Telerate (a supplier of live and historic price, rate and other information from the financial markets) to calculate a daily list of BBAIRS interest rate settlement rates and to publish this on its services. This constitutes a neutral and transparent method for fixing Libor.

Every day these rates are used for the floating leg in swaps. The rates are quoted for various maturities for each of nine currencies. You can access these rates on a Telerate screen at pages 3740–3750. They are also available on other screen services, such as Reuters.

Flexibility of Swaps

It must be clear that this type of transaction is extremely flexible. There are no prescribed or set contracts. Parties are free to agree on any terms that suit them. The permutations of these instruments are limited only by the imagination and by the availability of other parties who will agree to the terms.

Banks, which are the major creators of swaps, do in fact have various standard swaps available. They are created by the banks simply because there is such a demand in the market for swaps with certain structures. You will consequently find that your bank will have standard swaps available on which it can readily quote the available rates. Most of the time, these 'off-the-shelf' swaps will be adequate for your purposes.

The demand for swaps is great and the markets are extremely liquid. The counter parties are there. The limit is really your imagination driven by the needs of your business.

CHAPTER FIVE

Financial Options

Background

The term 'option' is well known to every businessperson. Yet as the term is used in the financial markets, it is necessary to analyze it quite thoroughly in order to understand exactly what is involved.

An option is such a widely used instrument that it cannot be pigeonholed easily into OTCs and exchange-traded options. The basic principles are universal to all options. There are changes of detail only when one investigates particular options, such as interest rate options. They do not change the universals, but some of the rules may vary. There are such things as interest rate caps and floors. These are multiple-exercise constructs built from the ordinary nature of options to suit particular needs. We will deal with these during the course of this discussion.

An option will often be the most easily available instrument to you in your business. It is a limited-risk instrument from the buyer's, or option taker's, point of view. Understanding the basic elements that are applicable to all options may well be the most rewarding time you ever spent on sharpening your business skills.

The Universal Principles of Options

An option is an agreement between two parties. One party gives the other party an option to do something. The giver of the option is, unsurprisingly, called the option giver, but more importantly, the giver is also known as the seller. Consequently, the person who is given the option is known as the option buyer. Prosaically, of course, the buyer is also known as the option taker and the option holder. The person taking the option obviously 'holds' it for as long as the option is valid.

Even in ordinary daily use, the term 'option' already says that the guy who has it has a choice, i.e. whatever the option may be about, the person holding it has a choice either to do something or not to do it. This, then, is the second and very important element of an option. The buyer of an option is given the right to do something, but she does not have the obligation to do it.

Assume you wanted to buy a house. You find a very attractive place at what you think is a good price, but you are unsure because you do not really know the market in that area. Maybe you would like to investigate the town planning schemes in that area to make sure the other party is not selling for some reason that you ought to know about; there may be plans that could have adverse effect on the value of the property. So you need a bit of time. On the other hand, while you are investigating, another buyer might snap up the deal in front of your nose. Your best bet would be to negotiate with the other party to give you an option to purchase the property at a price that both of you agree on.

The Rights Created by an Option Agreement – the Call Option

Let us consider the basic elements that are necessary to make the option deal a binding agreement. The first element to be agreed on is what rights are being given and taken. Using the above example of an option on a property, the right given would be the right to purchase the property. An option conferring on the holder of the option a right to purchase is known as a call option. In terms of such an option, the holder has the right to call upon the option giver to perform his obligations. As previously stated, the holder of the option has a right to do something – to purchase the property in this case – but not the obligation to do it.

The second element is that there must be an underlier to the option. An option is a right that refers to something else. In this case, it is a right to do something regarding a property. The property is the subject matter, the rationale, but more properly, the underlier of the option. In the option agreement, the underlier must be properly identified.

Buying or Selling Options versus Buying or Selling the Underlying

It is also pretty important to distinguish between the buyer and seller of the option as opposed to the buyer and seller of the underlier. The underlier is the property in our example. The option gives you the right to purchase the property. If you decide to take up the option, i.e. to exercise the right that it gives you, you will have a binding agreement of purchase and sale of the property between the two parties. In that resulting agreement of purchase and sale, the seller of the option is also the seller of the property. On the other hand, you, being the buyer of the option, are also the buyer of the property. In this case therefore, the situation is that the seller of the option is also the seller of the underlier, while the buyer of the option is also the buyer of the underlier.

The parties		The option buyer	The option seller
The right given	*Call option*	The right to buy the underlying	
	Put option	The right to sell the underlying	
The underlier		Anything that has commercial value	
The strike price		The price at which the underlier will be bought and sold in the event of the option being exercised	
The premium		The price paid by the option buyer to the option seller for the option	
Validity period		The period between the start of the option and the expiry date of the option	
Expiry date		The last day on which the option may be exercised	

The universal elements of an option

Table 5.1

This will not always be the situation. There is another type of option, the 'put' option, which turns the situation around. The put option is an option where the buyer of the option obtains the right to sell the underlier to the seller of the option. If this seems a little confusing now, don't worry. We will discuss a full example of a put option presently. Although our present example is a call option, the elements discussed are common to both option types (*see* Table 5.1).

Generally, we can say that in call options, the seller of the option will have the obligation to deliver the underlier, while the buyer will receive the underlier against payment of a previously agreed price. This latter element is the third element of an option, to which we now turn.

The Strike Price of an Option

The seller of the property will give you an option to purchase the property only if you agree on the purchase price of the property. Remember that he is bound by your decision. If you exercise the option, he has no right to deny you. He is bound hand and foot, while you enjoy the luxury of choice. In the agreement of option, therefore, the parties will state the exact price to be paid for the underlier should the option be exercised. This agreed price is known as the strike price – the price that has been struck for the underlier.

Period of Validity or Maturity of an Option

The fourth element is the period of the option. Nobody is going to give you an indefinite right to purchase his property. Because he is totally bound by what you eventually decide to do, he cannot deal with his property while you hold a valid option to purchase it. The parties will have to agree for what period the option will be valid. The option is therefore said to have an expiry date. If the option is not exercised by its expiry date, it lapses and is of no force or effect. The expiry date is an important concept in financial options. It is not only a specified date but also a specified time on that date. It is the last day on which the option may be exercised, up to the stated time of that day.

The Option Premium

The final and perhaps most problematic element is the option premium. It may be that you could get away without paying for the option in a residential property deal such as that used in our example, but in the financial markets a premium will always be due.

We can use our earlier residential property example again. Due to the option agreement, the seller is required to give up his right to dispose of his property at the first available opportunity. In so doing, he might lose an opportunity to sell and the market might move against him while he is waiting for you to make up your mind. He would place himself at this disadvantage only on condition that he gains something in the process.

The first thing he gains is at least the possibility of a buyer. But that is inadequate in terms of what he gives up. He will require value for value. You are also gaining an advantage. You will be able to reassure yourself on the factors mentioned earlier in the example; that represents value. Value given and value received must be paid for. The parties must agree on the premium to be paid for the option. The premium is paid at the beginning. It is paid when the option is given and it is not returnable if the option is not exercised. It is the price of the option.

The Rights Given by an Option – The Put Option

We have now dealt with the elements that apply to all options, but we have done so using the call option as our point of departure. Our example has also been that of a call option. Let us now consider the put option. Obviously if we can have an option that confers the right to purchase, the opposite must also be possible – there must be an option that confers the right, but not the obligation, to sell an underlying asset. This is called a put option.

If a put option is exercised, the seller of the option will be obliged

The parties		Puts	Calls
The buyer	*The right obtained*	The right, but not the obligation, to sell and deliver the underlier to the seller at the strike price of the option	The right, but not the obligation, to buy and accept delivery of the underlier at the strike price of the option
	The obligation incurred	To pay the premium	To pay the premium
The seller	*The obligation incurred*	Undertakes to buy and accept delivery of the underlier from the buyer at the strike price of the option, if it is exercised	Undertakes to sell and deliver the underlier to the buyer at the strike price of the option, if it is exercised
	The right obtained	To receive and keep the premium	To receive and keep the premium.

Table 5.2

The rights and duties of the sellers and buyers of call and put options

to take delivery of the underlier, while the buyer of the option will be obliged to give delivery of the underlier. *See* Table 5.2 for a comparison of call and put options.

Consider the case of a certain Arthur Jones. He acts as intermediary for a large property developing company that wants to build a major shopping complex in the London Docklands area. He is trying to purchase suitable smaller properties in the area, which will be consolidated and developed as one unit. He approaches Mr Patel who owns one of the properties. Mr Patel is not sure that he wants to sell. He is also not sure that the price is such a good one and he wants to investigate that aspect.

On the other hand, Mr Jones can buy other properties instead of Mr Patel's. They will serve his purpose equally well. Mr Patel would not like to miss a good deal if the present invitation proves to be a good one. The solution to his problem lies in negotiating an option. Here we have the opposite of the situation given in the first example.

Mr Patel wants to be given the right, but not the obligation, to sell his property to Mr Jones. If Mr Jones agrees to this, he will be unable to complete his property purchases before either Mr Patel has exercised his option or it has expired. This necessarily implies, as in the first example, that both a strike price and a period of validity of the option must be agreed to. Mr Jones will also require a premium to be paid in return for the time that he has to spend holding his horses. That is another matter they will have to agree on.

Option Pricing

The question that now arises is what the premium for an option will or should be. Option pricing has developed into a sophisticated mathematical discipline. It is an involved and esoteric but nevertheless fascinating subject, and there are extremely good textbooks available for the reader who is interested.

The easy answer to the question is, of course, that the market will determine the premium. While that is true, since the premium of any option is ultimately determined by market forces, the real question is actually: what elements will the market take into account in the process of pricing an option? A number of elements will play a role so it is also necessary to know what the relative force of each element will be in the whole process. The question is also what the interrelationship of these factors is.

This is a tough question. In the early 1970s, Fisher Black and Myron Scholes developed a mathematical model to predict option prices. Their work laid the foundation for options becoming the viable and popular instruments that they are today. The model has been a source of constant research and revision, yet it remains the basis of all modern option-pricing models. All good market analysis software packages include such an option-pricing model.

The value of an option must and will be reflected by its premium. 'Option value' and 'option premium' are often used interchangeably. Options are, of course, mispriced from time to time, thus affording arbitrage possibilities. A mispricing occurs when the option premium does not reflect the true value of the option. However, for the purposes of this discussion I will use the terms interchangeably.

A number of factors influence the value of an option. However, the total value is said to consist of two types: intrinsic value and time value. Before intrinsic value can be understood, we must discuss the relationship between the strike price or exercise price of an option and the price of the underlying.

The Price of the Underlying

The first factor that will be taken into account in the valuation of an option is the price of the underlier relative to the strike price of the option. The strike price, as you will recall, is the price at which the option holder will be able to either buy or sell (depending on the type of option) the underlier if he exercises the option. It is this relationship that will determine whether the option is in the money, at the money or out of the money.

An option in the money (ITM)
Returning to our first example of the option you took on that prop-

erty you were interested in buying, your investigation into the market value of that property could have revealed only one of three possibilities: either the strike price of the option (the price at which you could buy the property) was lower than the fair market value of the property, or it was equal to the fair market value, or it was higher than the fair market value.

If your investigation revealed that the strike price of the option was much lower than the market value of the property, it would mean you had a bargain on your hands. You could exercise the option and sell the house for an immediate profit. In this case, the strike would be said to be 'in the money' (ITM). The value of the option will be high. In fact, the option's value must at least be equal to the potential profit. In other words, the value of the option must at least be equal to the amount by which the market value of the property exceeds the strike price of the option. That amount is also the amount by which the option is said to be in the money. The amount by which the option is in the money is also called the intrinsic value of the option.

It follows from the above discussion that only an option that is in the money has intrinsic value. That is so because the intrinsic value of an option is by definition equal to the amount of money by which the option is in the money. All other options can therefore have only time value. As we will see, the actual value of an in the money option will even be higher than its intrinsic value because it also has time value.

An option at the money (ATM)
If the strike price of your option were equal to the fair market value of the property, the option would still have have a value, based on the factors that influence the time value of an option. Its value would obviously be less than its value would have been, had it been in the money. Under the circumstances, market parlance would have it that your option was 'at the money' (ATM).

An option out of the money (OTM)
However, if your investigation revealed that the strike price of the option you had been granted was higher than the market value of the property, the value of the option would be even less. Nobody is going to exercise an option to purchase a property for a price greater than its fair market value. The strike price would be said to be 'out of the money' (OTM). Therefore the option has a low value, but it is not worthless; it still has 'time value'.

Before we move on to discuss time value of an option, we must clear up any uncertainty about the use of terminology. Although it is the *strike price* of the option that may be in the money, at the money, or out of the money relative to the present price of the underlier, the convention is to refer to the *option* as being in, at or out of the money. Notwithstanding the fact that the strike price of the option is fixed for the duration of its validity, it is also conventional to refer to the option as moving into or out of the money. Of course, it is not the option or its strike price that moves, it is the price of the underlier.

Time Value of an Option

An option has time value because, during the remaining period of validity of the option, the market value of the property may rise. If it does, the strike price might yet become ATM or even ITM before the option expires. As long as there is a possibility of the spread between the market price of the underlier and the strike price narrowing, the option has value. Indeed, as the spread narrows, so its value will increase.

As we have already seen, an option must have value even if it is out of the money. Indeed, it is not only because the time period left to maturity may allow it to get into the money. An option that is already in the money may go deeper into the money, or it may move out of the money. Similarly, an option that is at the money may, over time, move into the money or out of the money.

We have already mentioned that an ITM option's total value will be greater than its intrinsic value. Taking the total value of an ITM option, its time value can be calculated by simply subtracting its intrinsic value. The total value of an ITM option, less its intrinsic value, must equal the time value. Time value is the only other value that an option can have. Therefore, the surplus value of an ITM option over its intrinsic value must constitute time value. That time value will be subject to the same influences that affect the value of ATM and ITM options. Do not think you can side step those factors by buying or writing ITM options.

These price and value movements of options take place over time. The possibilities of value changes exist within a time frame. Therefore, the markets can and will place a value on time. However, the time value of an option is not a constant. It is a very dynamic value that changes, often dramatically, over the period to the option's maturity. This is due to a number of factors that either give or remove the hope of profit. The hope of gain lies at the base of every factor in the market that influences value (*see* Table 5.3). We will now discuss the most important of these factors.

Time to Maturity

We have already said that the price of the underlier moves over time. The greater the time left until the expiry date (maturity) of the option, the greater the chance that its value may improve. It follows

		ITM options	OTM options	ATM options
Intrinsic value	*Call options*	The price of the underlier is greater than the strike price. The intrinsic value is the price difference	Nil	Nil
	Put options	The strike price is greater than the price of the underlier. The intrinsic value is the price difference	Nil	Nil
Time value	*Time to expiry*	The longer the time to expiry, the greater the value	The longer the time to expiry, the greater the value	The longer the time to expiry, the greater the value
	Market volatility	The greater the volatility, the greater the value	The greater the volatility, the greater the value	The greater the volatility, the greater the value
	'Risk-free' interest rate	The higher the interest rate, the greater the value	The higher the interest rate, the greater the value	The higher the interest rate, the greater the value
	Underlier price/ strike price differential	The further the option moves into the money, the less the time value, until the option reaches a delta of 1 – then it has no further time value	The closer the underlier price gets to the strike price, the greater the value	The differential is zero

Table 5.3

Factors that influence option premiums

that the more time to expiry, the greater the time value of the option. As its time runs out, so the time value shrinks. But the time value does not shrink linearly, although time to maturity decreases linearly. At the beginning of the life of an option its time value will diminish slowly, but the closer it gets to expiry, the faster its time value will approach zero (its value at expiry time on expiry day).

Do not let this argument fool you. You cannot infer from the above that the time value of an option will be at its greatest right at the start, on the first day of its validity. This is not necessarily so. The other factors that influence the time value of an option have such a major impact that the influence of time to maturity often becomes imperceptible. Not only that, its effect often seems to be turned on its head, reversed and generally ignored. Yet it is there, quietly gnaw-ing away at the values, exercising its subtle power. And in the end it wins, because when the option expires, its existence is terminated and its value is zero.

How deep OTM or ITM?

One cannot merely classify an option's strike relative to the price of the underlier as out of the money or in the money. Obviously, an at-the-money option is either at the money or it isn't. An out-of-the-money option, however, can be nearer or further out of the money. The same applies to an in-the-money option. How near to the money, how far out of the money or how deep into the money the option is has a profound effect on its value.

It follows, therefore, that the closer the price of the underlier is to the strike price of an OTM option, the greater will be its time value. The price movement required to take it into the money is so much less. Also, the deeper an option moves into the money, the greater its time value becomes. Obviously, the price movement required to take it out of the money is so much greater. Therefore the chances that it will move out of the money become less and less as the time to maturity shrinks and the option moves deeper and deeper into the money.

When you purchase an option, you will notice how the value of that option changes as the price of the underlier moves towards, away from or through the strike price.

Market Volatility

Clearly, the time value of an option is based on the probability of the option getting into a better position *vis-à-vis* the price of the under-lier. Although the amount of time left will increase that probability, the volatility of the price of the underlier will also be a determinant.

When we discussed market volatility under measuring risk, we pointed out that volatility itself is a variable. We also said that the greater the volatility the greater the risk. In the markets evaluation of an option, the volatility coin is looked at from the other side. The greater the risk, the greater the opportunity. In other words, the greater the volatility in the underlier's market, the greater the chances are that its price will hit the strike price of the option. Therefore, we can say that the higher the volatility in the underly-ing markets, the greater the time value of the option.

Whenever you purchase an option, you will notice from the daily market reports that as the volatility of the underlying market goes up, so the value of the option will increase. When the volatility of the underlying market dies down, the value of your option will deflate.

The impact of the volatility phenomenon on option values is so great that it has given rise to speculators indulging in what is known as volatility trading. Many traders are of the opinion that it is easier to call the direction of market volatility than to call the overall price movement of the market. When volatility rises, the premiums of all options at all strikes increase, and when volatility falls, the premiums of all options at all strikes tumble. These traders consequently buy options when volatility is low and sell when volatility is high.

Market volatility is a definite factor that you should consider when you purchase an option. You are a hedger. You want to avoid paying an inflated option premium simply because of high volatility in the market. On the other hand, high market volatility, with its concomitant risk to your business, may be exactly what drives you to hedge. Then you must accept that the price of your hedge will be higher. The price of not hedging would likely be even higher.

The 'Risk-Free' Interest Rate

The final factor that influences an option's value is the price of money. Because time is such a valuable element of the value, it follows that the time value of money must also be factored in. The 'risk-free' interest rate during the period of the option's currency is the rate that is used by most option-pricing models.

The Greeks

A lot has now been said about the value of an option and why it changes during its currency. We need to know, however, *how* the value of an option changes during its currency. How do all the factors that we have discussed interact to give us a value from moment to moment? This question brings us to the Greeks.

The great Homer said: '*Timeo Danaos et dona ferentes*' ('I fear the gift-bearing Greeks'). The gifts that these Greeks bring however are not to be feared. They do not bring Trojan horses but rather knowledge that can be used to our advantage.

We already know that the value of an option does not change by one unit for every one unit that the price of the underlier changes. Yet whenever the price of the underlier changes, the premium, or value, of the option changes with it. What is the relationship?

The Mathematical Relationship

Options really only became viable market instruments once the mathematical models were established and the proper premiums for options could be calculated. The development work of Black and Scholes still forms the basis for calculating the value of options.

Delta	The change in the value of the option for every one unit of change in the price of the underlier
Gamma	A measure of how much the delta of an option changes for every one unit of change in the underlier
Theta	A measure of the decay of the time value of an option, per given period, over the life of the option
Vega	A measure of the change in the value of an option for a 1 per cent change in the volatility of the underlying market

Table 5.4

The definitions for each of four Greeks

A number of mathematical equations are built into option pricing models to describe the price relationship between options and their underliers. These equations are known as 'the Greeks' because they have (mostly) been given names of letters of the Greek alphabet. The most important ones are delta, gamma, theta and vega, although this last one has nothing to do with the Greek alphabet. Table 5.4 gives the basic definition for each of the terms.

The Option Delta

The major Greek that concerns us is delta, sometimes referred to as 'the hedge ratio'. It is a variable ratio that changes as the price of the underlier changes. Its value can be anything between zero and one. An option that is deep in the money has a delta of one. An option that is ATM will have a delta of .5, while an OTM option's delta will be close to zero. How the delta of an option changes with a change in the price of the underlying, is illustrated in Figure 5.1.

The delta value of an option therefore means that an option with a delta of 0.5 will change in value by only half as much as the underlier will, for the entire price move of the underlier from that point onwards. The value of an option with a delta of one will react one-on-one with the underlier, i.e. its change in value will move linearly with the change in value of the underlier. As an example, consider the premium of a call option with a delta of 0.25. Its value will increase by only 25 per cent of the increase in value of the underlier. At the same time, while the value of the underlier increases, the option is getting closer to the money. The closer it gets to the money, the higher its delta becomes. It is for this reason that the delta value of an option describes an 'S' curve when plotted against the value scale of the underlier.

The implications and opportunities for using delta in the business of hedging will become clear in later chapters.

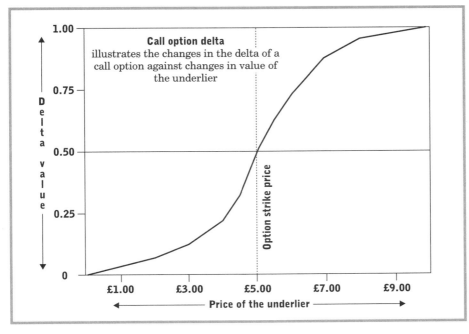

The delta curve of a call option

Exercising an Option

It almost goes without saying that it is only the buyer of an option that can exercise it, precisely because it is the buyer or holder that is given the choice. Exercising an option naturally brings the life of an option to an end.

In the financial markets, only an option that is in the money can be exercised. If you think about it, why would somebody want to exercise an option that gives him a worse price for the underlier than he can get by simply doing the transaction on the underlying market?

European and American-Style Options

There are two styles of option – American and European. An American-style option can be exercised at any time during its currency. Whenever the option is in the money, the holder can exercise it. By contrast, a European-style option can be exercised only on its day of expiration, on condition that the option is in the money. Whenever you buy or sell an option, make sure you know which style of option you are dealing with because it has an effect on the risk.

The seller of a European-style option is at risk only on the expiration day of the option, while the seller of an American-style option is at risk at all times during the life of the option. American-style options are more popular and give much more flexibility. However, they are more expensive than European-style options.

The result of exercising an option

When you exercise an option, or if it is automatically exercised at expiration, you end up long or short the underlier, depending on whether it was a call or a put that you exercised. If you exercise a call option, you will be assigned a long position in the underlier. You will be long the underlier at the strike price of the option. This means that you will be a buyer of the underlying at the strike of the option. You will then have to pay the price and accept delivery of the underlying. If you do not wish to possess the underlying, you will be able to avoid that only by immediately selling it. By doing so you will also realize the profit that is represented by the amount by which the option was in the money when you exercised it or when it expired ITM.

If it was a call option on a futures contract, you will be assigned a long futures position. This will become clear when we deal with futures contracts.

If you exercise a put option, you will be assigned a short position in the underlier. You will be short the underlier at the strike price of the option. This means that you will be a seller of the underlying at the strike price of the option. You will then have to deliver the underlying against receipt of the price. If you do not already possess the underlier, you will immediately have to buy it at the current price. In doing so you will realize the profit that is represented by the amount by which the option was in the money when you exercised it or when it expired ITM.

If it was a put option on a futures contract, you will be assigned a short futures position. The implications of this will become clear when we discuss futures contracts and their options.

Assume for a moment that you wanted to exercise a call option on certain stock. In order to do so, the present price of the stock must be higher than the strike price of your option. Your option must be ITM. You have already paid the premium for the option and now you will have to pay for the stock as well. The amount you will pay for the stock is the strike price of the option. Your total cost of acquiring the underlier will therefore be an amount equal to the strike price of the option, plus the premium of the option.

Once you have exercised your call option and paid the price, you now have the underlier at your disposal. But the show isn't over yet because you have a choice. You can either hold on to the underlier in the hope that it may have a further gain in value, or you can sell it immediately to make a profit. If you hold on to it, it is, of course, at the risk that it may lose value again.

Before exercising an option, you should always consider whether it is deep enough into the money to cover the premium that you paid. When the option is in the money to the same amount as the premium paid of it, it is said to be at breakeven. You are obviously not making a profit before the option moves deeper into the money than breakeven. It does not make sense to exercise an option that is not at least at breakeven, unless it is only slightly in the money and it is nearly expiration time on expiration day. At that time you may as well exercise the option to mitigate your losses.

Depending on whether they are exercising a call or a put, traders often put in an order to buy or sell the underlier at the same time that they exercise the option. The opposite position that is thereby taken on the underlier then automatically cancels out the position in the underlying that is assigned on the exercise of the option.

Holding an option to expiry

There are decided risks when you hold an option to expiry. The purpose of the discussion that follows is merely to make you aware of these risks so that you will take due care when holding an option.

We know that an option places no obligation on the seller. He can walk away from it. However, you do not wish to walk away from an option that is ITM. From its exercise you could at least have recouped all or part of your premium, not to mention having realized a tidy profit if it was deep in the money. Apropos to that, I can offer only the few thoughts that follow.

When you buy options, the old adage of *caveat emptor* (let the buyer beware) applies, albeit in a somewhat unusual context. When you buy an option in your business, at the very least you must make sure that you note its expiration date. Second, when you own an option the onus is on you to monitor its value at all times. Unless there is automatic exercise at expiration, never, ever allow an in-the-money option to expire – exercise it timeously. If you do not exercise an ITM option before expiry, you will lose the total advantage of having bought it. This is true of all over-the-counter options.

The situation can be even more serious when it comes to certain exchange traded options and options on futures. Many, if not all, of these exchange-traded options have automatic exercise if it expires in the money. On futures exchanges, all options that expire in the money are automatically exercised. You have to watch this situation very carefully because if your option is ITM and it is automatically exercised, you are going to have a position in the underlying that will need your immediate attention.

Profit and Loss at Option Expiration

As we have seen, an American-style option can be exercised if it is ITM at any time. Yet most American-style options, and of course all European-style options, survive to expiration. We now have to investigate what the holder's profit or loss situation is when he holds an option to expiration.

During the life of the option, as we have seen, the value of the option is problematical. It is not so at expiration – the value is zero. However, the financial result at option expiration is simple to calculate. Then it is not the value of the option we are concerned with but the immediately realizable value that is locked in the underlying, less the premium paid.

Figures 5.2 to 5.5 illustrate this position. Consider that they show the situation only at the exercise of the option or at option expiration. They do not take into account the price changes of an option during its period of validity. They therefore assume that the option itself has no value.

The four figures already take into account the premium paid for the option. Figures 5.2 and 5.3 illustrate the realizable value in the hands of the option holder for a whole range of values of the underlying asset. It is assumed, therefore, that the call option holder purchases the underlying asset and the put option holder sells the underlying asset at any one of the indicated prices, while at the same time the option expires or it is exercised.

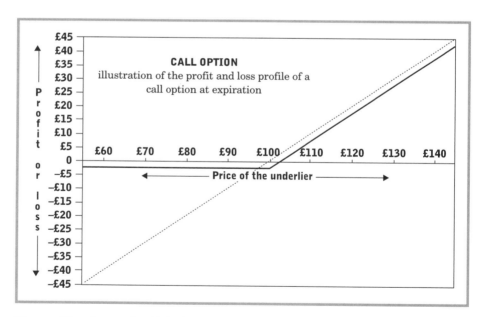

Figure 5.2

The profit or loss potential of the buyer of a call option for all values of the underlier, at expiration of the option

Figure 5.2 is self-explanatory. It illustrates a call option buyer's profit/loss situation at option expiration for a range of values of the underlying. Figure 5.3 illustrates the same situation with a put option.

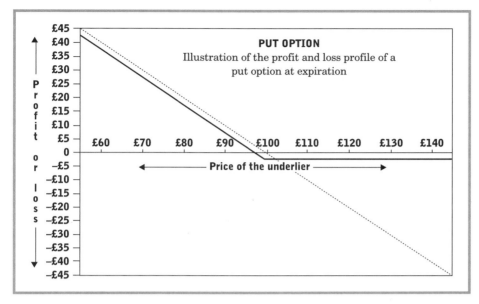

Figure
5.3

The profit or loss potential of the buyer of a put option, for all values of the underlier, at expiration of the option

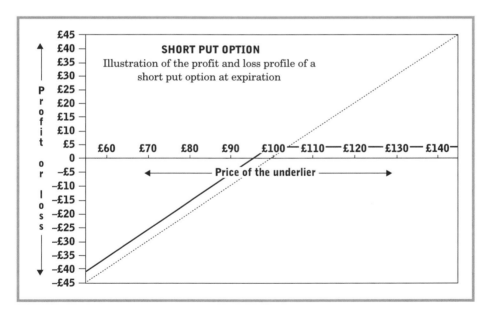

Figure
5.4

The profit or loss potential of the seller of a put option, for all values of the underlier, as at expiration of the option

Figures 5.4 and 5.5 illustrate the situation from the put and call option seller's point of view. In all of the figures the profit/loss profile of the option is compared with the profit loss/profile of holding the underlying asset if it had been purchased or sold at the strike of the option concerned. The latter profile is indicated by the dashed line.

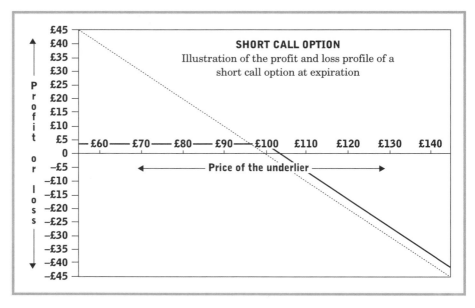

The profit and loss potential of a seller of a call option, for all values of the underlier, as at expiration of the option

The figures all illustrate the difference between the strike price of the option and the value of the underlying at the time of expiry of the option. As previously stated, the option itself has no value at expiration because it no longer exists.

Looking at these figures, first note that the amounts reflected on the respective *x*- and *y*-axes are merely illustrative and do not represent any real option price structure. This is because it does not matter what figures are used. Real or imaginary figures, the shape and meaning of the lines remain the same. It also does not matter whether we are talking about over-the-counter or exchange-traded options – the analysis remains equally valid.

For the purposes of all the figures the strike price of the options is assumed to be £100. The solid line indicates the profit or loss of the option holder, read against the *y*-axis, that will be gained or lost from the underlying market, read from the *x*-axis, given the option strike price and the premium paid or received, as the case may be. The broken line illustrates the profit/loss profile of an imaginary linearly linked variable, such as a futures contract, if it had been bought or sold at the strike price of the option.

Profit/Loss from Long Options

Value that will be gained or lost from the underlying market means the profit that could immediately be realized on the underlying market. Consider Figure 5.2 for example. This illustrates the profit/loss profile of a long call. 'Long' as always refers to something that has been bought. In this case it reflects the situation of the buyer of a call option. The strike price of the option is $100, while the option premium was $2.50. Taking any value from the figure, let us assume that at the time the option expires, the value of the underlying is $115. If the holder exercises the option, or if it is automatically exercised, he will be assigned the underlying asset at a price of $100. He will be able to sell it immediately for $115, realizing a gross profit of $15, less the premium, giving him a net profit of $12.50. This net value is what the dotted line in the figure indicates.

In Figures 5.2. and 5.3 notice how the solid line runs parallel to and below the x-axis. This remains its position right up to the strike price of the option. The parallel portion of the solid line indicates the values of the underlying for which the option holder will show a loss at maturity. Reading on the y-axis, one can determine the cost or premium of the option. The premium of the option equals the maximum loss that the buyer can make on the option. The line then makes a sharp turn and runs parallel to the linear-risk line into positive territory. All the long options show a loss right up to the strike price.

The important thing to note is that it does not matter how far the price of the underlier moves in an adverse direction – the loss remains the same. When the price of the underlier moves favourably beyond the strike price, the option is in the money. The loss starts by narrowing, then reaches breakeven and thereafter becomes a profit as the favourable price move of the underlier continues.

Profit/Loss from Short Options

Figures 5.4 and 5.5 have legends that include the term 'short'. The terms 'short call' and 'short put' are the easiest way of conveying that the figure illustrates the position of an option that has been sold, not bought. 'Short' is the market term for selling a thing, anything, and is often used as a substitute for the verb 'to sell'. Someone who sells an item without possessing it is therefore said to be short that item. The same analysis for the long options also holds good for the short options. Notice however, how they show a flat profit profile but a descending loss profile.

The short options show the reverse profile of the long options. Notice in both figures how the solid line stays in the profit region right up to the strike price and then falls away into the negative as the price of the underlier moves adversely. The profit remains the same for all values of the underlier right up to the strike price. This is because the premium collected is the only profit that the seller can show. If the underlier does not move adversely, his profit remains the same.

One advantage that the seller has is that his profit is not dependent on how big the price move of the underlier is, but only on the direction in which it moves. If, during the currency of the option, the price of the underlier does not move much at all, or if it moves only further out of the money, the seller of the option gets to keep all the premium. The buyer's profit, on the other hand, depends not only on the direction of the underlier's price move but also on the size of the move. In a low-volatility market, prices may move steadily in one direction, perhaps into the money as far as a particular option is concerned, but the move may be so small that the resultant profit is hardly worth the investment. This is not the primary concern of a hedger, however.

Although there are advantages to being the seller of an option, the above demonstrates again that the seller of an option has a limited profit potential, while the risk is virtually limitless.

Profit and Loss Potential

From the figures, we see that the profit potential of long options and the loss potential of short options are linear to the price of the underlier. We can also say that the two values are positively correlated. However, this is true only for the moment of expiration. During the currency of the option, it is a different matter. Then, as we have shown, the value of the option will fluctuate.

Option Multiple Exercise Constructs – Caps and Floors

In the marketplace you are going to find many terms that may be confusing. A number of terms have developed that are specifically used in the OTC markets. When one deals with options in the interest rate market, one is confronted by terms such as 'lenders' options' and 'borrowers' options'. These are merely substitutes for interest rate calls and interest rate puts respectively.

Apart from changes and differences in terminology, you will also find different option products. These special option products have developed especially in the OTC markets. They are commonly used in the interest rate, currency and commodity markets. They are really a series (also called strips) of shorter-term options, all with the same strike price, that have been packaged together as one longer-term option with a strike price equal to the strike prices of the shorter-term options. Of course, a premium is due.

Strips of call options are called caps, while strips of put options are called floors. Each short-term option that forms part of a cap is called a caplet, while the equivalent option in a floor is called a floorlet.

The Needs Addressed by Caps and Floors

The need for these specially constructed products arises from two basic circumstances. The first is the exercise conditions of European-style options. As we know, the distinguishing feature of European-style options is that they can be exercised only at expiration. For both the writers and the holders, they create risk only on expiration date. For risk purposes, it is only relevant whether such caps and floors are in the money or out of the money on expiration date.

This latter feature is an extremely useful and advantageous one. Most risks that a business might be exposed to have periodicity, i.e. the risk may not be continuous for the whole period of exposure. The whole period will usually be divided up into a number of shorter periods.

The Advantage of Periodicity in Options

As an illustration, consider a business with a two-year bank loan. The interest is fixed quarterly in advance and payable quarterly in arrears. Any change in the interest rate can therefore take effect only at the start of any one of the three-month periods, or quarters, into which the total loan is divided.

The interest rate that takes effect at the start of any quarter can obviously not be any historic or anticipated rate. It must be the interest rate that is the market rate for the next three-month period as it is fixed on that starting date. In other words, if any particular quarter started on, say, May 1, the three-month Libor fixing at 11 a.m. on May 1 would be the rate used to fix the rate of the loan for the next three months.

It follows that the risk that this particular business faces is an adverse three-month Libor fixing on the start date of any three-month period, as defined by the terms of the loan. Interest rate movements in the interim are really irrelevant to the risk. The business in fact has a loan with a term of two years but with a three-month risk periodicity.

If interest rate risks have periodicity, it is only natural that derivative instruments with matched periodicity would be created. We have dealt with swaps, which have such periodicity in the cash flows that are swapped. Swaps do not have premiums, while a premium is due on a cap or a floor, as is the case with all options. Against that however, there is a duty in a swap to transact, but an option confers a right without any obligation to transact. It follows that one instrument will sometimes be more advantageous to use than the other.

However, options are single-period instruments. The answer is, then, to link a number of sequential options as caplets or floorlets. They each have an identical strike and thus form a chain of options that, taken together, cover a longer period of risk exposure as a single option with multiple settlement.

You can imagine that similar risk periodicity also arises for investors periodically rolling over their investments. It obviously also applies to importers and exporters of goods who have periodic currency payments to meet, as well as to regular purchasers of a commodity who make buyers of the same commodity over long periods of time. These chains of options are therefore growing in popularity, especially in the interest rate, currency and commodity markets. As far as commodities are concerned, the present market is centred on oil.

The due dates of the shorter periods are referred to as exercise dates or as rollover dates.

Structure of Caps and Floors

Caps and floors are cash settled. This means that the principal amount of the underlying is never exchanged. The principal is merely notional. A cap will protect the holder against a rise in the price of the underlying at each of the multiple exercise dates over the agreed period, while a floor will protect the holder against a fall in the price of the underlying on the same basis.

This means that at each one of the multiple exercise dates, the price of the underlying will be compared to the market price of the underlying. In the case of a cap, should the market price of the underlying be higher than the strike, the writer of the cap will pay to the holder the difference between the strike price and the market price. The difference in price will be calculated over the period of the caplet. A floor works in the same way, except that the writer of the floor will reimburse the holder at each exercise date if the market price is lower than the strike price of the floor.

In other words, we can say that a cap 'caps' the price of the underlier at the strike price. During the validity of a cap, the holder will never have to pay more for the underlying than the strike price. A floor, on the other hand, establishes a floor price for the underlying. It guarantees that, for the life of the floor, the holder will not have to sell or invest at a lower price than the strike price of the floor.

The situation is illustrated in Figure 5.6. Here, neither the holder of the cap nor the holder of the floor would have been reimbursed during the whole period. Although the underlier's price moved above and below the respective strikes at some stage, it was always either above the strike of the floor or below the strike of the cap at every rollover date. If the rollover date had coincided with the rollover dates of a hedged risk, neither of the parties would have suffered any disadvantage.

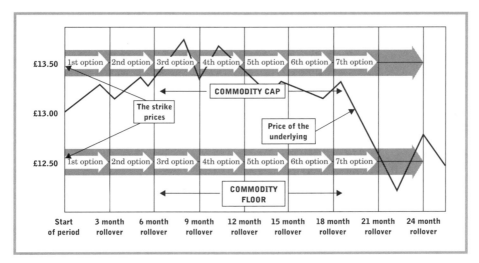

The structure of a cap with a strike of £13.50 and a floor with a strike of £12.50

Figure 5.6

We will now consider interest rate caps and floors, currency caps and floors, and commodity caps and floors (*see* Table 5.5). Each of these instruments has its own peculiarities, all as a result of the implications of linking strings of options.

Interest Rate Caps and Floors

The cap or floor is for a notional amount of money. Unlike most ordinary options, it is not for a quantity of the underlying. This is because the underlying is merely an index and therefore has no quantitative value unless it is based on an amount of money.

The underlying of an interest rate cap or floor is an interest rate index, such as any period of Libor. The result of this is that at every rollover date the current applicable Libor fixing is compared to the strike of the cap or floor. Payment of the difference, if any, is made by the writing bank to the holder. The difference that is paid to the holder is calculated by deducting the one interest rate from the other and then multiplying the result by the notional principal.

When the strike price is determined at the start of the cap or floor, it is done with reference to a benchmark interest rate. One would expect the benchmark to be the current applicable Libor fixing, but it is not. Because of the long period involved, the current swap rate is used as the benchmark. In other words, the cap or floor will be ITM, ATM or OTM with reference to the current swap rate. As we already know, this factor will be the major determinant of the premium, together with all the other previously mentioned factors that influence option premiums.

	Interest rate caps and floors	Currency caps and floors	Commodity caps and floors
Notional principal	An amount sounding in money	An amount sounding in money, denominated in a currency linked to the underlying	A quantity of a commodity linked to the underlying
The underlying	Any interest index, such as three-month Libor, six-month Libor, etc.	Any exchange rate index for the two currencies concerned	Any standard price index for a commodity, such as a *Platt's* index price for oil and fuel
Benchmark price	The swap rate for the underlying against which the strike rate is fixed at the start	The swap rate for the underlying against which the strike rate is fixed at the start	The swap rate for the underlying against which the strike rate is fixed at the start
The strike rate	The rate to which the underlying index rate is compared at every rollover date	The rate to which the underlying index rate is compared at every rollover date	The rate to which the underlying rate's average for the past period is compared at every rollover date

Table 5.5

The basic elements of caps and floors

Currency Caps and Floors

These instruments do not differ in principle from the interest rate caps and floors. There will be a notional amount of principal, denominated in one of the two currencies involved. That quantity of currency will play a role in determining the premium of the option. Since the underlying is a rate of exchange, the notional principal serves to quantify the risk and the payout if the option is ITM.

The underlying will be the rate of exchange between two specified currencies. Any index can be used that suits the parties. The difference between the strike and the index rate will serve as the basis for the payout, if any, at every rollover date during the life of the cap or floor. As in the interest rate instruments, the benchmark rate will be the swap rate of the two currencies at the time of the fixing of the strike of the cap or floor.

Commodity Caps and Floors

In this case, the quantitative value of the cap or floor will be based on a notional quantity of commodity linked to the underlying of the instrument. If this sounds strange, it is because there is not actually a commodity that underlies the instrument. The underlying of a cap or floor will always be a rate or a price index. It will never be a physical product or commodity. However, in the case of a commodity cap or floor, the price index will be the price index of a particular commodity. For example, the relevant commodity may be bunker fuel, but the actual underlying of the cap or floor will be a specific price index of the commodity, such as *Platt's* Bunkerwire Rotterdam IF 380.

As in the previous two cases, the strike price will be determined with reference to the swap rate of the commodity at the time when the cap or floor is negotiated by the parties. The benchmark is thus the swap rate.

The procedure on every one of the multiple exercise dates however, differs from the procedure in the previous two instruments. At every rollover date the average price of the underlying index is compared to the strike rate of the cap or floor. In a cap, if the average index price for the commodity for the period between rollover dates was higher than the strike price, the writer of the cap will pay the difference, calculated on the notional quantity of the commodity. This type of cap or floor, where the average price is compared to the strike, is often also referred to as Asian options.

Such a departure from procedure obviously has an impact on risk. The cap or floor could be for a period as long as seven years, although the norm is between two and five years. The net effect of the procedure is however, that for the whole period of the instrument, the holder will be compensated for such amount as the average price of the commodity during that period exceeded the strike price of the cap or floor. This means that the risk is a continuous one.

Contrary to the position with all other caps and floors, it is not the price at rollover date that is the risk, but the average price for the period. The effect of having a string of sequential caplets or floorlets is thus that the compensation is eventually for the average price for the commodity over the whole period of the cap or floor. The cap thus 'caps' the average price of the commodity at the strike of the cap, for the whole period of the cap. Alternatively, it establishes a floor price for the average price of the commodity at the strike of the floor, and the holder of the floor will not have to accept any lower price for the commodity during the period of its validity.

The hedger, in this case, does not have to go to great lengths to ensure that the periodicity of the rollovers matches the periodicity of his purchases. These are therefore ideal instruments to counter commodity price risks where the hedger makes regular purchases at unpredictable times.

Availability of Energy Caps and Floors

As is the case with commodity swaps, the big players in this market are the major oil companies as well as the banks. Energy caps and floors are available in relatively small quantities of 1,000 barrels of crude and 500 metric tonnes in the case of oil products, making them accessible to the hedger who requires only smaller quantities. These instruments are becoming increasingly popular, resulting in a very acceptable level of liquidity.

The Risk Created by Caps and Floors

The risk that is created by a cap for its holder is the risk that the price of the underlying will be less than the strike price of the cap at each rollover date. In that event, the cap can never be exercised and the premium paid for it will be lost. This premium is the maximum loss that can be suffered.

The risk that a floor creates for its holder is that the price of the underlying remains above the strike price of the floor on every rollover date. If the floor cannot be exercised during its period of validity, it lapses. The premium paid for the floor will be forfeit, again the maximum loss that the holder can suffer.

The risks are therefore the same as for call and put option holders. Sellers, as in all option products, have limited rewards (the premium received), but their risk is limited only by how far the price moves against them. Theoretically, their losses are thus unlimited.

The Risk of the Parties to Options

In the business of hedging our main concern is, as always, the risk. Only when we know what the risks are will we be able to use options to get the desired results.

The Buyer's Risk

The first order of investigation is the risk incurred by the buyer of an option. If you purchase an option, you pay the premium. If the option you purchase is out of the money or at the money, you can do one of two things – either wait until expiration or sell the option at any opportune moment during its currency. Some options are freely transferable, while others can be sold back to the seller only for 'fair value'. Fair value can be nothing other than the market price of the option determined according to the factors discussed above.

During the time that one holds an option, its value is going to change. It can change up or down, depending on the price movement of the underlier and the volatility of the underlying market. The value of the option that is due solely to time will decline at its normal pace, accelerating the trend as it moves closer to expiry. If you wait until expiration of the option, its value will be zero. The value of an option will be zero only at expiry because then it no longer exists. The buyer therefore runs the risk that he may lose the entire premium paid. This represents his bottom line.

But it is not necessary for the buyer to lose the entire premium paid. Depending on all the circumstances and the legal terms of the option, he can sell it on to a third party or back to the seller before it expires. The timing of this action will obviously depend on the state of the underlying market and the resultant changes in the value of the option.

As against his risk, he has unlimited upside potential. He can profit from a change in price by as much as the market allows that price to change, less the premium paid. Although that is generally true, there is a theoretical limit to how much profit a buyer can make on a put. Consider that the put allows the buyer to sell the underlier at a certain price – the strike price. The profit he can earn is determined by how much the market price is lower than the strike price of the option at the time that he exercises it. Since the market price cannot go below zero, the limit of a put option buyer's profit is equal to the difference between the strike price of the option and zero. Because there is very little chance of the underlier's price ever reaching zero, the actual profit limit is lower.

The Seller's Risk

The risk that the seller faces is of a different order altogether. The seller irrevocably gains the premium and need never give it back. If the price of the underlier moves against him, he will lose the full value of that move, less the premium received.

The seller of a call option, for instance, will lose money the moment the price of the underlier begins to rise. Keep in mind what was said above of how the values of options change. The seller of the call will begin to lose money only once the price of the underlier exceeds the strike price of the option he sold. The option will start gaining in value the moment the underlier's price moves upwards. The same holds true for the seller of a put. The option starts gaining value the moment the price of the underlier moves down. The seller of a call and of a put option is always at risk that the option will gain in value after he has sold it. *See* Table 5.6 for a comparison of the risks assumed by the parties to options.

The above holds true whether one has sold a call or a put. A put option will gain in value if the price of the underlier starts moving down. This means that the underlier is becoming cheaper, while the seller of the put has undertaken to buy the underlier at a fixed strike price. The closer the price of the underlier gets to that strike price, the more valuable the option becomes. Once the price of the underlier has fallen through the strike price of the put option, the option is ITM. If the seller were now called upon to fulfil his part of the bargain, he would have to buy the underlier at the strike price, which would be higher than the market price. He would be saddled with something that he could get rid of at a loss only.

The parties		Call option	Put option
The buyer	Profit potential	Unlimited on the upside	Limited to the difference between the strike price and zero
	Risk	the full premium paid	The full premium paid
The seller	Profit potential	The full premium received	The full premium received
	Risk	Unlimited on the upside	Limited to the difference between the strike price and zero

Table 5.6

The risk/reward profile of the parties to options

CHAPTER SIX

Commodity Futures

Background

Commodity futures are the final tool of the craft. Once you learn how this tool works, you will be able to enjoy all the advantages that the business of hedging holds. It is probably the easiest of all the tools to use and to understand. They only trade on futures exchanges and all the rules and regulations pertaining to each futures contract is fully disclosed by the exchange that it is traded on.

The futures contract developed naturally out of the forward agreement, when, about 150 years ago, people involved in the agricultural sector in the mid-western states of the US came to realize that there were shortcomings in the well-established forward contract.

Development of the Futures Contract

The major shortcoming of the cash forward contract was to be found in the credit risk that the parties incurred. Sometimes the farmer would quite happily deliver his crop to the buyer who had bought forward his crop, only to discover that the buyer was unable to pay as promised. On the other hand, the farmer's crop often did not come up to expectations and he could not deliver as agreed. This left the buyer having to scramble at the last minute to try to find more inventory to meet his requirements.

In addition, there was no transparent price discovery. Nobody was ever sure whether the price they were getting for their produce, or the price they were paying, was really a competitive market price. The experience in Chicago was typical of many other places. Immediately after harvest, the farmers would bring their crop to market. Everybody would be there. This would cause a tremendous oversupply of agricultural produce, especially of grains. The glut would cause prices to plummet. The low prices would discourage farmers from selling their produce and eventually a good proportion of the grain crop was dumped in the St Lawrence river before disgruntled farmers returned to their farms to try again the following year. The dumping of large portions of the crop caused shortages later in the year, but that was of little use to the farmers. There was thus great instability in prices and in supply. The markets were continuously in chaos. It was either a flood or a famine. Clearly, a better system was required.

Then somebody had a bright idea. It involved three basic innovations on the forward contract. The first was the creation of a standardized contract, enabling it to be traded on an exchange. The second was that the contract would be freely negotiable, or on-sellable. The third was that credit risk would all but disappear.

As a result, farmers in the American Midwest and agricultural merchants based in Chicago started the first futures exchange 150 years ago. That exchange still exists as the Chicago Board of Trade (CBOT) and it is one of the world's great exchanges.

During the development of the futures contract over the years that followed, some further distinctions between forwards and futures became apparent, because, despite the drawbacks, cash forward agreements never fell out of favour. They are still very much alive and well and are used frequently and effectively, not only in agriculture, but in every financial market. They are extremely valuable instruments in risk management. Whereas the forward agreement is an instrument that allows parties to contract out of price risk, the commodity futures contract is an instrument that creates price risk and allows parties to hedge. Hedging proved to be one of the greatest advantages of futures exchanges. It is estimated that today, the greater part of trades that are done on futures exchanges are done with the purpose of hedging.

Some Basic Features of Futures Contracts

Some of the basic features of a futures contract have become apparent from the discussion so far. In the first instance, in order to have a standardized contract, the terms and conditions of the agreement must be pre-specified by the exchange on which it trades. The only outstanding contractual term that the parties have to agree on must be the price. This structure allows the contract to be traded on an exchange, which operates as an auction on the exchange floor.

Benefits of an Exchange

This begs the question of what the benefits of trading contracts on an exchange might be. Constructing a standardized contract to make it exchange tradable would serve no purpose unless there were great advantages to be gained from trading the contracts on an exchange. In fact, exchange trading bring substantial advantages. First, it creates a transparent price discovery mechanism. It also allows contracts to be traded with delivery dates staggered into the future. This in turn obviates the chaotic situation created by effectively having only one delivery month – harvest time. Spreading delivery of the crop over a number of months obviously creates greater consistency in supply and demand. The flood-or-famine type of situation is thus avoided.

The Futures Price

As we have said, with a standardized contract only a fair price needs to be established. The price, of course, reflects the market expectation of the price of the underlying commodity at the specified future delivery date, given today's market conditions. When the price of futures or the futures price is referred to, it is really a reference to the anticipated price of the commodity.

In fact, it is incorrect merely to refer to a futures price for a commodity. There is no such thing as a futures price as such. We must always refer to the price of futures of a commodity for a particular delivery month. We can refer to the December price of corn futures or the March rate for US dollar/Swiss franc futures. If, on occasion, one does encounter a reference merely to the futures price of a commodity, it is a reference to the near futures month for that commodity. The near futures month is the first delivery month of futures from now, whenever 'now' may be.

The basis of the futures agreement, like any other agreement, is the undertaking of mutual rights and obligations by the buyer and the seller. The buyer undertakes to take delivery of, and pay the agreed price for, the underlying commodity on a specified future date. The seller undertakes to deliver the underlying on that specified date against receipt of the contract price.

The price the parties have to agree on is the price of the underlying at that specified date. In addition, all rights and obligations created by the agreement lie in the future. If you are the buyer in a futures contract, you do not pay anything now; your obligation to pay the contract price lies in the future. Similarly, if you are the seller in a futures contract, you receive nothing now and you deliver nothing now. Your right to receive the contract price and your duty to deliver the underlying lies in the future.

People trying to get to grips with futures often ask: 'How can I buy a futures and not pay anything?' They also ask: 'How come I sell the futures, but I don't get any money for it?' Let us get the terminology clear. Although the previous paragraph sets out the legal situation correctly, this is not the language of the market. In the market, you are said to 'buy' or 'sell' a futures contract. Of course, you are not buying or selling a contract. The futures contract, unlike an option, is not an instrument that is assigned a value. When you 'buy' a futures contract, you are actually taking up the position of a buyer in a contract of purchase and sale of the underlying commodity or instrument. Similarly, if you sell a futures contract, you are taking the position of a seller of the underlying for future delivery.

Market Terminology as used in the Futures Markets

In market terminology, the buyer of the futures is also said to be long the futures or to hold a long futures position. The seller is said to be short the futures or to hold a short futures position. The terms 'go long' and 'go short' are also directly substituted for the verbs 'to buy' and 'to sell' respectively. One might therefore say that one goes long one futures contract, instead of saying that one buys a futures contract. Similarly, a trader might say 'I shorted ten futures' rather than saying 'I sold ten futures contracts'.

Take note that one does not need to be long a futures contract, or to possess the underlying, in order to sell a futures contract. You may initially take a long or a short futures position, just as you wish. If you start by taking a short futures position, you will have to go long the futures later, in order to close out your original short position. Alternatively, you can hold your short position until delivery date. Then you will have to deliver the underlying to the exchange, which may involve having to buy in the underlying commodity on the spot market. The point to keep in mind, though, is that there are no restrictions on selling futures, such as you have on bear trades on a stock exchange. No pre-conditions or regulations exist in the futures markets that limit or control bear trades.

We are now ready to discuss the three basic innovations of the futures contract. The principles discussed are applicable to all futures contracts. It does not matter whether the underlying is corn, pork bellies, interest rates, crude oil or equity indices – the basic principles and working of their futures contracts are exactly the same. It is only in specifics, such as the actual contract conditions, contract size, price quotes, delivery processes and so forth, that one futures contract differs from another.

The Three Innovations of the Futures Contract

The three innovations we are looking at are innovations on forward agreements. None of them is unique in itself. The combination of the three gave rise to a separate market, the futures market, which operates side by side with the spot market.

The market is, however, not merely an extension of the spot market. It is a financial derivatives market that is linked to the cash market through the delivery mechanism. It is not a market that is aimed at the person or firm that wishes to trade in the underlying commodity or instrument. Financial stability and risk management are the true purpose of the market.

The three innovations that gave rise to futures contracts were first, the introduction of a contract with standard terms and conditions that trades on an exchange, that, second, is freely negotiable, and third, in which credit risk is virtually eliminated.

The Minimum Standard Terms and Conditions

In order for a futures contract to be viable, a certain minimum number of standard conditions need to be prescribed. Any number of other and further conditions may be included in an exchange's specifications. The standard conditions of any particular futures contract will be found in the contract specifications published by the exchange on which the contract trades (*see* Table 6.1) .

The Underlying, Basis Grade and Deliverable Grades

The first standard condition of any futures contract is a full description of the underlying, i.e. corn, wheat, oil, treasury bonds, etc. The description needs to be very specific. The exact type of corn, wheat, oils and so forth will be specified along with the grade. This specified grade is known as the basis grade of the contract and this is the only grade that may be delivered in terms of the contract. However, in some instances exchanges do allow a lower grade to be delivered at a discount, or a higher grade at a premium. Such variations will form part of the contract specification.

The Contract Size

The second important condition is the size of the contract. This is the quantity of the underlying which is traded in each contract. The parties cannot select the quantity of the underlying for which they contract – they can decide how many contracts they wish to buy or sell, but the quantity traded with each contract is fixed.

The Delivery Month

The price the parties have to agree on is a price that they think will be fair value for the underlying at a particular date in the future. Therefore, that date is an essential element of the agreement and it constitutes the third basic standardized condition of a futures contract.

Every futures contract trades for delivery of the underlying at a specified time in the future, but delivery is never set only for a particular date. Rather, delivery is stipulated to take place at any time during a period between two specified dates. Delivery periods always fall within particular calendar months. The same months will be used every year for each particular contract. For this reason the futures contracts are always referred to by the delivery month of the

Standardized contract	The underlying
	The basis grade of the underlying, as well as acceptable premium and discount grades, if any
	The contract size – 5,000 bushels, 1,000 ounces, etc.
	Contract delivery months
	Predetermined points that are 'regular for delivery'
	Price quote – cents per bushel, dollars per ounce, etc.
	Miscellaneous provisions – tick sizes, trading hours, etc.
Freely on-sellable	Interposing the clearinghouse – a seller to all buyers and a buyer to all sellers
	The offsetting mechanism
Elimination of credit risk	Guaranteed by the clearinghouse
	The margin requirement

Table 6.1

The three innovations of the futures contract

contract. For example, a trader may say that he wants to buy March corn, or another might say he wants to sell December wheat. By this, the former means that he wants to buy futures contracts with corn as underlier for delivery in March, while the latter wishes to sell futures contracts with wheat as underlier for delivery in December.

The first date for delivery in a month is important. After that date the holder of a short futures position may be called upon to deliver the underlying, while the holder of a long position may be called upon to take delivery of the underlying.

In the contract specifications, the exchange will designate the delivery months that are available for each underlier. The traditional delivery months, a legacy from the agricultural past, are July, September, December, March and May. Many of the newer futures contracts for non-agricultural commodities have delivery dates in every calendar month.

The Delivery Process

The fourth element of the standardized contract is the delivery process. The contract always specifies how and where delivery of the underlying will be accepted. The seller never delivers the underlying directly to the buyer. He always delivers to the exchange at a place that is 'regular for delivery'. The buyer always takes delivery of the underlying from a place and in a manner prescribed by the exchange. Although delivery plays a vital role in any buy/sell agreement, let it be said immediately that a futures exchange is not a place where people come in order to purchase the physicals. The futures market is a financial market and the physicals, or underlying, is traded on the spot market. The mechanism that allows a participant in the futures market to get out of his obligation to deliver or to take delivery of the underlying is called offsetting.

The delivery process plays a significant role in the price mechanism, but physical delivery seldom takes place. It is because delivery is possible in terms of a futures contract that the spot price of the underlying and the price of the futures will always trade in a certain relationship to each other. This will be explained anon.

There is a further process known as exchange for physicals (EFP). This allows a party who is short futures to exchange the physical underlying with a party who holds a long futures position. This exchange leaves each party to deliver or obtain the underlying asset while extinguishing their futures position. EFP's are, however, transactions negotiated between parties directly and are not done on the floor of the exchange.

The Price Quote

The final basic element that we need to discuss is the price quote. Every contract has a prescribed way in which the price is quoted. On the Chicago Board of Trade, for example, corn is quoted in cents per bushel. Each commodity has its own style of price quote. Price information makes no sense unless you know the price quote style and the size of the contract. Since the CBOT corn contract size is 5,000 bushels, a price quote of 125¢ for CBOT corn would tell us that the value of one corn futures contract for that delivery month is $6,250 (125/100 x 5000).

Some Incidental Provisions

There are numerous other incidentals which are usually also specified in a futures contract, trading times and tick sizes being two of them. A tick size is the minimum amount that the price can increase or decrease by in any bid or offer. In other words, if somebody has put in a bid and you want to improve on it, you cannot bid just any amount. The higher bid or lower offer must be at least one tick above or below the previous one. Any bid or offer must be an amount that equals a multiple of one tick. As an example, one tick in the CBOT corn contract is 5¢. Only bids and offers in multiples of 5¢ are allowed and any bid must improve on the previous one by at least 5¢.

Having constructed a standardized contract, it could now trade on an exchange. The first innovation on the forward contract is complete. The next innovation is to arrange things in such a way that a futures contract that had been entered into on the exchange will become freely transferable, or on-sellable, to third parties.

Contract Negotiability or On-Sellability

The basic problem with contract negotiability is a legal one. Understandably, any agreement entered into is not transferable by one party without the consent of the other party. If you were the seller of a particular thing for which payment still had to be made, you could not allow me, as the buyer, to transfer my rights and obligations to whoever I wanted to as you might not appreciate the creditworthiness of the person I foist upon you.

The opposite is equally true. The buyer would not wish to have another seller thrust upon him. He might not trust the new seller to give him the same quality; he might not trust him to perform his obligations. So making a contract freely negotiable presents a very real problem.

The Clearinghouse

The solution to the problem lay in the establishment of a clearinghouse and the process of 'setting off'. Every futures exchange is affiliated to a clearinghouse, which is the financial heart of the exchange. All transactions that are done on the floor of an exchange are reported daily to the clearinghouse, which then 'clears' the transactions. In 'clearing' the transaction, the clearinghouse actually records the transaction, connecting the two parties to the transaction to each other. They must establish that, in the first instance, a transaction was actually done. That means that for every transaction there must be a buyer and a seller. Then they determine the margins that have to be deposited by each party as at the end of that trading day and net the margins that they require each member firm to deposit or to receive. Don't worry about this process now, the margin situation will be made clear below.

The clearinghouse, having determined that there are counter parties at a particular price for every trade, then interposes itself between those parties. It becomes the seller to all buyers and the buyer to all sellers. Thus, a party transacting on a futures exchange is not concerned in any way with the identity of the counter party with whom he is striking a particular deal. The parties are anonymous to each other because their identities, creditworthiness, net worth and so on mean nothing to the counter party. One party will not be looking to the other for performance; in fact, a party will be looking at the clearinghouse of the exchange to fulfil the counter obligations of the agreement.

By means of this arrangement, the legal bond has been shifted from the party with whom the bargain has been struck to the clearinghouse. The parties are no longer legally bound to each other for performance of the contract. Each party is legally bound only to the clearinghouse. This vastly improves the credit risk, but it does not quite eliminate it. When we deal with the workings of margin, we will see how the risk virtually disappears. The stage is now set for the contract to become on-sellable to third parties without the other party's consent. This process is known as setting off.

Setting Off

In order to demonstrate how a party would set off its position on a futures exchange, let us consider the following example. On September 14, a fund manager in Los Angeles purchases, or goes long, 50 S&P 500 futures contacts on the Chicago Mercantile Exchange (CME). The manager enters the transaction because he is hedging. The other party, who is the seller of the contracts, is a speculator in New York. She is doing the deal because she believes the index is going to fall. Obviously, each party is unaware of the other party's identity and intentions. Nor do they care. On September 20, the index has gained 20 points. The Los Angeles fund manager now wishes to lift the hedge at a profit. The New York speculator does not want to abandon her position even though she is making a loss. She still believes the index is going to make a strong downward move.

On September 20, the fund manager enters an order to sell, or short, the 50 contracts. On the floor of the exchange a buyer is found who happens to be a private investor from London who is speculating on a further upward move of the index. The LA fund manager has now closed out his position for a profit of 20 index points. The New York speculator neither knows nor cares about this transaction.

When the transaction is reported to the clearinghouse at the end of each trading day, it notes that the fund manager was an existing long (a person holding a long position is often referred to as 'the long'). It also notes that he has now gone short the exact number of contracts in the same delivery month that he was long. His long and short positions therefore cancel one another out, so that the fund manager is now out of the market. The clearinghouse is left with the new London investor, but no seller to link him to because the person who sold to him has just short-circuited himself out of the market. On the other hand, the New York speculator is hanging around in the books without a buyer because her original buyer has been eliminated from the market through the deal with the London investor. Obviously, the clearinghouse can substitute the London investor as the buyer in the contract in which the New York speculator is a seller. The parties, who are now linked to each other in the books of the clearinghouse as buyer and seller, did not transact with each other at any stage. Added to this is the fact that they each transacted at a different price. All of this is irrelevant. Because of the interposition of the clearinghouse, it must balance its books to reflect that for every contract, called an open position, there must be a buyer and a seller.

Although the offsetting mechanism makes getting out of a futures position look easy, it must be stressed that the obligations in terms of a futures contract are serious. Any person who holds a long position in futures beyond the first delivery day prescribed by the exchange may be obliged to accept delivery of and pay for the underlying. He will be obliged to pay the price agreed upon when he entered his long futures position – not the price of the underlying at the time delivery is given. A person holding a short position in futures beyond the first delivery day will be obliged to deliver, when called upon to do so, the underlying to the exchange as provided by the standard terms of the contract. Against delivery, the short will be paid the original price that the futures contract was entered into on the exchange when the short position was taken. He will not be paid the spot price of the underlying that is current at the time of delivery.

The risk of holding on to a position too long must therefore be clear. When you have open positions on the futures market, you must always be keenly aware of the delivery dates. Set off the positions timeously in order to avoid dealing in the physicals. Use the futures only for hedging and deal with the underlying on the spot market.

The Creation of Open Positions

As long as there is a buyer and a seller in a contract on which performance is still outstanding, an open position exists. The positions are referred to as 'open' because the parties have not yet fulfilled their obligations. They did enter into an agreement, so a contract does exist. Their rights and obligations, however, lie in the future. Therefore they have not yet had to perform them and the contract is open to performance. Open positions are created by new buyers and new sellers coming into the market and contracting with each other. The number of open positions is consequently a factor of demand and supply for the contract in each delivery month. The number of open positions is recorded for every contract in every contract delivery month.

It follows that there will be a different number of open positions in a contract for every available delivery month of that contract. Obviously, the demand for a particular commodity, such as heating oil, will be greater in December and January than in any other month. The December heating oil futures contract will therefore usually have more open positions than the heating oil futures for May delivery.

Open Interest

The total number of open positions in a contract for each delivery month is reported as the open interest in market data reports. The open interest in any contract informs us what the present demand for a commodity is for delivery in any particular month in the future.

Open interest changes from day to day. By following the open interest figures, market analysts can determine some trends in the marketplace. We must not think that open interest only increases; it decreases as well. Here we are not referring to a decrease due to performance of the contract. Obviously open interest will decrease to nothing as the delivery month of the contract ends. Open interest can remain level, even if the contract trades, and it can decrease notwithstanding continuous vigorous trading. Open interest will remain stable when people who leave the market by offsetting their positions are equal to the newcomers. It will decrease when people who hold positions in the market leave by offsetting their positions in greater numbers than there are newcomers entering the market. The changes in open positions constitute important information for traders who rely heavily on market data.

The structuring of the exchange in such a way that the clearinghouse is interposed between the parties, coupled with the clearing mechanism that allows the on-selling of futures positions, completed the innovation of contract negotiability. We will now look at how the final innovation, the elimination of credit risk, was successfully implemented.

The Elimination of Credit Risk

Due to the legal interposition of the exchange's clearinghouse between the parties to a futures contract, the credit risk of a party is really related to the risk of non-performance by the clearinghouse. Credit risk has been shifted to the risk of dealing with the clearinghouse. The members of the clearinghouse must be financially strong and competent. The creditworthiness of the exchange is actually the creditworthiness of the clearinghouse.

All industrialized countries have stringent rules controlling exchanges, their clearinghouses and their financial requirements. The whole business of futures trading is highly regulated to protect the user of the facilities. The rules and regulations have been developed over many years and have proven extremely effective in protecting the public. In the developed world, thus, one can say that the credit risk you incur by dealing on a listed futures exchange through registered brokers is negligible. This is enhanced by the provision of margin.

Margin Requirements

As we have said, interposing the clearinghouse between the parties drastically reduced credit risk, but of course the clearinghouse would be subject to the credit risk of the parties trading on the exchange. If the financial wellbeing of the clearinghouse were to be endangered by vast numbers of risky trades on the exchange, the whole system would be endangered. A system was therefore devised requiring margin deposits to protect the clearinghouse as well as, in the final analysis, the trading public making use of the exchange.

Every member of an exchange has to have a margin account with the clearinghouse. Margin is an amount of money, determined from time to time by the exchange, which a member of an exchange is required to have on deposit with the clearinghouse of that exchange for each futures position taken up. The money is held in the margin account of the member firm. This may be too simplistic a definition, but we can use it as our point of departure.

Notice that it is a requirement of the clearinghouses that is applicable to members of the exchange and not the trading public who may be clients of the member. The clearinghouse therefore never deals with the trading public. It is exposed to the credit risk of its members only. This is the first risk-reducing factor. The second factor, inherent in the definition, is that the money must already be held on deposit before the member will be allowed to enter the trade. It is the member firm's responsibility to ensure that its clients' obligations to it are at least as onerous as its obligation to the clearinghouse. It is also the member firm's responsibility to ensure that the client honours the obligations.

There are three levels of margin. These are determined by the exchange from time to time, depending on circumstances (*see* Table 6.2). The margin that needs to be held on deposit at the time of the trade is called original margin. It is obviously held by the clearinghouse as a security deposit. The margin requirements are assessed by the clearinghouse on a continuous basis, according to the volatility of the market at any stage. The higher the volatility, the higher the risk and, therefore, the higher the margin. It is not the policy of clearinghouses to adjust margin requirements continuously. They will try to hold them as steady as possible. Therefore, there will usually be an adjustment to margin only when there is a substantial jump in market volatility. When volatility goes down, the margin requirement for that contract will be adjusted downwards again to the normal, published level. The published margin requirement is based on the historic volatility of a contract and it will never be adjusted to below that level.

There is one variation on original margin that interests us in the business of hedging. Most exchanges have a lower margin requirement for hedgers. The reason for this is that the hedger represents a lower risk to the clearinghouse than speculators. You will not always qualify as a hedger, even if your purpose is to hedge. If you are a user or producer of the underlying, you will be registered as a hedger for the purposes of dealing in contracts relating to such commodities. If you are registered and you trade futures contracts in the relevant commodity, you will be required to comply only with the lower requirement of hedger margin. This matter should be taken up with your broker at the time that you appoint the firm. It will arrange for your registration as a hedger in any particular underlying commodity or commodities for which you may qualify as a hedger.

The next level of margin is known as maintenance margin. Some smaller exchanges do not have maintenance margin requirements and insist on original margin being held in the account for as long as the position is held. Generally, exchanges have a different margin requirement if a position is held 'overnight'. If a position is not closed out, or offset, by the end of the trading day, the amount of margin required to hold the position will be a lesser amount than the amount of original margin. This lesser amount is what is referred to as maintenance margin. Maintenance margin is required to maintain a futures position, as opposed to original margin that is the margin required to take up a futures position.

The third level of margin is called variation margin. This varies with the price of the underlying. At the end of every trading day, the clearinghouse determines the settlement price of every futures contract traded on the exchange. At that time, the clearinghouse compares the margin deposit of the member firm with the settlement price of the futures contract. If the price of the futures has changed adversely for the member, the amount of the adverse change is debited against the member's margin deposit account. The result will be that the member firm has too little margin on deposit. The clearinghouse will now call upon the member firm to deposit more money into its account to bring it to the level of the original margin required for the position. In other words, if there is an adverse movement in the price of the futures, variation margin is required to bring the margin deposit up to the level of original margin and not to the level of maintenance margin. The fact that the position is held overnight does not influence this situation. Only if a position is held overnight and no adverse price movement has taken place does the margin requirement reduce to the level of maintenance margin.

The converse is also true. If there has been a favourable price change, the margin account of the holder of that position is credited with the amount of the change. Variation margin therefore represents money that can flow out of or into a margin account, based on the price movement of the futures contract involved.

Original margin (lower for hedgers)	The amount that an exchange requires to be held on deposit before a futures position can be taken in a particular contract
	It will be increased with an increase in market volatility
	It will differ for each contract, being based on the historic price volatility of each contract
Maintenance margin	A lower amount of margin to be held when a position is maintained 'overnight'
	It is only applicable if no adverse price movement in the futures has occurred
Variation margin	An amount that varies with and is equal to the price movement of the futures
	An adverse price movement will require payment of margin to bring the account to the level of original margin
	A favourable price movement will cause an inflow of money equal to the movement in price

Table 6.2

The three levels of margin

Let us look at an example. Assume that a metal merchant sells copper futures on the Comex (the metals division of the New York Mercantile Exchange). A speculator in metals takes the opposite position. The contract size is 25,000 lb of copper and the price quote is US cent per lb. Original margin is $2,000 and variation margin is $1,500. The merchant sells ten contracts at 75.70¢ and deposits $20,000 in her margin account. The speculator buys ten contracts at that price. He also deposits $20,000 in his margin account. At the end of that day the price of copper settles at 76¢.

The total value of the ten contracts was $189,250 (75.7¢ x 25,000 x 10) at the time the parties entered the futures. At the end of the trading day the total value was $190,000.00. Both parties hold their positions overnight. The price move reflects a loss for the merchant of $750.00 and a profit for the speculator of $750.00. For the purposes of all examples, we will ignore commissions and other trading costs, which do not affect margin.

The metals merchant will now receive a margin call for $750.00, which amount she will have to deposit before the start of trading on the following trading day. The speculator will receive an amount of $750.00, paid into his margin account. This money will be withdrawable funds because they are in excess of the original margin required. He will now be required to have only $15,000 margin in his account, but the additional $5,000 in the account because of the original margin of $20,000 that was initially paid in does not represent withdrawable funds. The $5,000 is, however, available for use as margin on further positions.

Each party's margin will be adjusted in this way at the end of each trading day for as long as such party holds his or her position. Notice how the mechanism neatly manages the credit risk. The debit and the credit were originally entered by the clearinghouse against the margin accounts of the broking members. They are required to hold large margin accounts with the clearinghouse, which will ensure that sufficient funds are always available to cover more than one day's trading. The result is that both the merchant and the speculator are not exposed to credit risk due to the financial condition of their respective brokers. The clearinghouse covers for them and for itself by holding large sums on margin deposit from these firms.

Analyzing the example, it is plain that the broker for the metal merchant has to rely on the merchant to pay the $750 the following day. However, he is adequately covered because he still holds a margin deposit of $19,250 from her. Should she not pay the required amount timeously and should the broker no longer trust her, his bottom-line plan of action is to liquidate her position immediately, deduct the losses and his fees from the deposit he holds, and pay the balance out to her.

You can imagine that the total margin is large enough not to fall prey to losses easily. It would require an extraordinarily tardy broker to allow prices to move so far against a client that the margin he holds becomes insufficient to cover the losses. Should he be so negligent, it will be his loss. His losses will not affect his other clients or for that matter, the clearinghouse.

With the implementation of the margin mechanism, credit risk was all but eliminated. In addition, strong government controls and regulation of every aspect of the futures industry in the developed world help to ensure ethical standards, good conduct and sound management practice by all concerned.

The risk of trading on the futures markets are therefore limited to the risk incurred through the positions taken in futures and their price movements resulting from the operation of market forces. We can now move on to a discussion of the price mechanism and how it operates in the futures markets.

Pricing the Futures

We have already noted that the price of commodity futures will always trade in a certain relationship to the cash, or spot, market. The economic link is the fact that the physical commodity is deliverable against the futures contract. Were it not for this element, there would be no link between the two markets and futures prices would drift aimlessly. In fact, it is to be doubted whether there would be any futures trading – if there were no link between the spot and the futures markets and therefore no particular price relationship, the futures would serve no purpose. Keep in mind that futures are derivatives. Their prices are therefore derived ones – from the spot price of the underlying.

Having said that, you should also bear in mind that the price of futures is not linearly derived from the spot price. The spot price is the price for immediate delivery of the underlying, while futures prices are for future delivery. Futures contracts trade for different delivery months into the future and each projection further into the future has cost implications that will be discounted into the futures prices. By necessary implication, this means that the futures price for the contract with the nearest delivery month will trade at a different price to the spot market.

Our point for time reference when we refer to futures and spot is always right now – the moment that we say these words. The spot market is therefore the 'now' market. You will recall that when we discussed delivery months for futures contracts, we mentioned the standard delivery months of March, May, July, September and December. The delivery months will vary according to the underlying commodity, but at least the above months will be available. Before you trade any futures contract, you must get a copy of the contract specifications. Virtually all exchanges keep a Web site and the contract specs can be accessed and downloaded from there.

The Spot Price

The first element to be considered is the price of spot, although the totality of the cash market of the underlying, which has a bearing on futures prices, must also be taken into consideration. Remember that futures contracts trade on an open market. Nobody determines or calculates the price of futures, it is determined solely by market forces such as supply and demand for a particular futures contract. The matter under discussion now is which factors will influence the market in reaching a particular price for a particular contract.

Two important cash market conditions are relevant to the price of futures. The first is what is known as a normal market, while the second is known as an inverse market. Both of these are conditions of the cash market, but because futures are derivative instruments, these conditions will obviously play a decisive role also in the determination of the futures price.

Normal Market Conditions

Normal market conditions are found when there is no particular shortage of a commodity and when supply is plentiful. These conditions therefore apply when supply, relative to demand, is anywhere from adequate to a glut. Supplies are then regarded as normal. There is no panic in the market since everybody can readily obtain whatever supplies of the commodity that are required at the time that they are required.

Under normal market conditions, the spot price will be the lowest price. The spot price, being the price of the commodity for immediate delivery, is the 'now' price. The nearest futures delivery month's price will be higher, and every following delivery month will have a slightly higher price than the previous one. The stepped price into the future is the result of the cumulative carrying costs. For this reason, a normal market is also referred to as a carry-cost market.

Carrying cost refers to the cost that would be incurred if you had to purchase spot silver and hold the physical for a month. Obviously it would cost money to hold the physical commodity. The monthly carrying cost includes monthly interest on the spot price, storage and insurance for one calendar month.

To illustrate the situation, let us examine the example shown in Figure 6.1. Assume that 'now' happens to be August 1 and that the

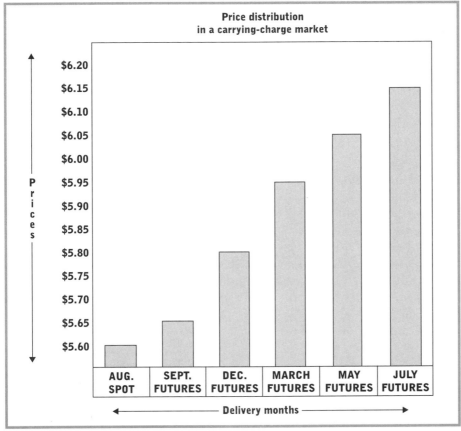

Figure 6.1

The maximum price differential between spot and deferred months, given a carry of 5¢

spot price of silver is $5.60 per ounce. The first bar in the figure indicates this situation. Assume further that the carrying cost for silver is 5¢ per ounce per month. Taking the 5¢ carrying cost as a given, the maximum price that September futures can be is $5.65 ($5.60 spot + 5¢ carry), while the maximum price of December futures will be $5.80 ($5.60 spot + 20¢ carry for four months). The maximum prices for the further deferred months are indicated by the other bars in the figure.

The Trading Relationship of Spot to Futures and of Near Futures to Deferred Futures

Consider a manufacturing jeweller in Amsterdam that wishes to purchase 5,000 ounces of silver. He knows that he will require the silver in one month's time, but the present spot price suits him and he is concerned that silver prices are on the rise. He can now enter the spot market, pay $5.60 an ounce and store the silver for a month. The total cost to him would be $5.65 per ounce. Before he buys the spot, he checks the price of the nearest month's futures and sees that it is trading at $5.63 per ounce. By immediately buying the nearest futures instead of the spot silver, he will save himself 2¢ per ounce. This also demonstrates why a person who requires a commodity in the future would rather purchase a futures than buy it on the spot market and hold it in inventory. The precise advantage and mechanism of this use of futures will be explained fully when we deal with hedging. This example price differential will fall into normal parameters, given our assumptions.

What would happen in the converse situation? Let us say the nearest futures were trading at $5.70 per ounce, while spot was trading at $5.60. Sellers of silver on the spot market would not sell. They would all sell futures and hold the physical silver for a month. They would incur costs of 5¢ per ounce and forego the $5.60 that they could have obtained in the spot market. If they were to sell the futures and deliver the silver on the futures contract, their net price, after allowing for the carry, would be $5.65 per ounce. Their realized price would earn them an additional profit of 5¢ per ounce over the price they could have obtained a month earlier, after allowing for the carry.

A speculator would be in an even better position. If you were a speculator, you would purchase the physical silver on the spot market at $5.60 and immediately sell the futures contract at $5.70. Knowing that the one-month carry will be 5¢ per ounce, you would then take delivery of the physical silver that you bought on the spot market and promptly store it for one month. Having now incurred a carry of 5¢ per ounce for the month, this cost has to be added to the $5.60 per ounce you paid. Your total cost for the silver would therefore be $5.65 per ounce. Against that cost, you have already made a sale of the silver for delivery in one month's time, at a price of $5.70. You would realize your profit after one month by making delivery of the silver through the delivery process of the futures exchange. This type of trading is known as arbitrage trading.

The same logic applies to price differences between one futures delivery month and a following or deferred futures delivery month. If the December futures were trading at $6 while September futures were trading at $5.65, the premium to December would be 35¢, while the carrying charge for three months (September 1 to December 1) would amount to only 15¢. A trader on the look-out for such mispricing would immediately buy September futures and sell an equal number of December futures contracts. The trader would take delivery of the physical silver through the futures exchange delivery mechanism and accept the carrying charge of 15¢. At the very moment the trade in futures was made, the trader made a risk-free profit of 20¢ per ounce (35¢ representing the price differential between the two contract months minus 15¢ for three months' carrying charges).

Some traders are so finely tuned to such mispricing that they can immediately take advantage of the situation. They are known as arbitrage traders. They make a business out of arbitrage trading because mispricing does occur from time to time, but such occasions are rare and exist for moments only. Arbitrage profits are risk-free.

Now, consider what would happen to market prices due to the action of these sellers and arbitrageurs. First, because of the heavy selling pressure on the nearest futures contract, its price would drop. Second, due to the absence of sellers on the spot market, the buying pressure would cause the spot price to rise. The result of this interaction would be that the two prices, spot and nearest futures, would quickly fall back into line.

From this example it is clear that, in a normal market, the futures price can never be greater than the spot plus carry. If it were, market forces would react immediately and bring the high price down, while bringing the lower price up at the same time. However, this is not the same as saying that in a carrying-charge market the price difference into the deferred months will be equal to the carrying charge. It is merely a fact that the difference cannot be greater than the carry. In fact, the price differences will rarely be as great as the carry. It is most likely that the price of the nearest futures month will be slightly less than the carrying charges and this trend will continue into the deferred months.

We must note a single condition here. The situation discussed above reflects the market in non-perishables. Where the underlier is a perishable, such as eggs, there is a danger of spoilage. It will therefore not always be possible to hold and store the underlier against a sale for future delivery, since there is a real danger that the goods may no longer be in a deliverable condition. Therefore, in perishable commodities, the premium of the deferred futures month's price over the near month, and the near futures month over spot, is not limited to carrying charges. The premium can therefore exceed carrying charges by any margin that market conditions will allow.

The Convergence of Spot and Futures Prices

There is one other fact that we can learn from this discussion. During the delivery month of a futures contract, the spot price and the futures price will tend to converge. In other words, in the delivery month of a futures contract the market conditions that influence the spot price will be nearly the same as the conditions that influence the futures price. The carrying charge will become less and less as the period to the final delivery day of the futures delivery month shortens. The carrying charge will obviously be zero on the last day for delivery. The price differential will therefore tend towards zero because the carrying charge tends to zero. When carry is zero, for the reasons discussed above, the futures price cannot exceed spot by more than zero.

Although perishables are an exception to the carrying-charge rule, they do not represent an exception to the price convergence rule. As the period to final delivery day on futures shortens, so the likelihood of spoilage lessens. This process will continue until the period to final delivery equals the safe period for storage of the perishable. At that stage, the normal considerations of a carrying charge market will apply to that perishable. Therefore, in the futures delivery month, the spot price and the futures month's prices of perishables will still converge and tend to zero.

The Inverse Market

The other type of market condition that we must look at is the inverse market. We have noted that this condition pertains when there is a shortage of the underlier. Buyers aggressively buy as much of the physical as they can lay their hands on. This action causes the spot price to rise. Next, they will buy as much on the futures market as they can get sellers to sell. The nearer futures delivery months will have greater buying pressure than further months because market participants will usually believe that the shortage is temporary. When shortages do occur, appropriate action is usually taken to relieve the shortage. Markets therefore usually believe that the shortage will be short-lived and will last only until supplies are transported in. As a result, the spot price will be greater than the nearest futures, while deferred futures will trade progressively lower (*see* Figure 6.2).

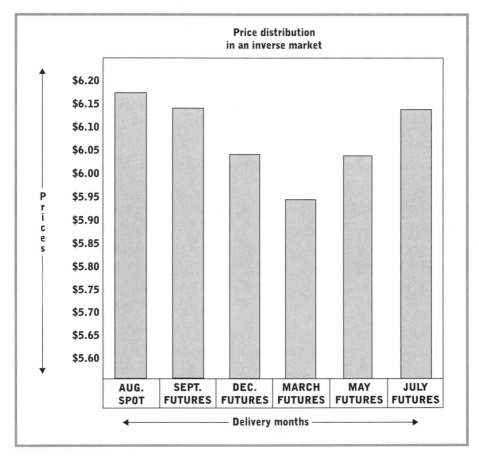

**Price distribution
in an inverse market**

**Figure
6.2**

A possible price distribution scenario in an inverse market

Taking the illustration in Figure 6.2 as an example, we can see how high the price of spot is relative to the level of deferred prices. This clearly demonstrates a shortage of the underlying commodity in the cash market. You can see that September and December futures are also under some considerable buying pressure. Clearly, the market expectation in August is that supply and demand for the underlying will stabilize in March. Compare Figures 6.1 and 6.2. It is clear that there is no real buying pressure on the deferred months of March, May and July. They reflect a normal carrying-charge market.

There is no way to profit from the price disparity found in inverse markets. No market mechanism therefore exists that will automatically drag prices back into line. The premium that spot can have over near futures and near futures over deferred futures is consequently unlimited. We should look at the reasons for this phenomenon.

It is trite to say that in the business of buying and selling, profits are only possible when you buy low and sell high. Consider the fact that the reason why the price disparity in a normal market can be used for profit is that the nearer month is cheaper than the further month. Therefore you can buy low now, take delivery, and sell at a disproportionately higher price into the future. In this way you profit from the mispricing.

If one tried to profit from a price situation where the near month had the higher price, you would have to sell in the near month (high) and buy in the deferred month (low). Although you may legally sell something now that you will acquire only in the future, you cannot deliver now something that you will acquire only in the future. The problem is that the arrival of the delivery date of the near month would require you to deliver the physical product because you are a seller. If you did not possess the physical at the time you were required to deliver it, you would be forced to buy it in on the spot market. In the delivery month of the futures, the spot price would be close to the price of the futures, but that would be as high or higher than the price you actually sold at in the deferred futures month. This transaction is doomed to failure.

Notice again that the spot price of the commodity and the futures price will tend to converge in the futures delivery month, even in an inverted market. This is because the market pressures on spot and futures will resemble one another closely during the delivery month.

The Basis

This is an extremely important concept in futures, which cannot be emphasized enough. The reader is urged to commit the principles discussed to memory and to absorb them totally. This is core knowledge. In the business of hedging, basis and its movement is germane to the whole process. A proper understanding and a full appreciation of basis are essential requirements of successful hedging.

In general, the term is used to describe the price difference between spot and the nearest futures contract. Using the example discussed in the previous section, you will recall that spot silver was trading at $5.60 on August 1. Assume that September futures were trading at $5.63 and December futures at $5.76. The basis for silver would be said to be 3¢ under ($5.60 spot − $5.63 futures = −$0.03 basis). This is just a way of saying that the spot price was 3¢ under the futures price. The basis is always expressed as a relation of spot, or cash, to futures, never the other way round. If September futures were trading at $5.50 against a spot price of $5.60, the basis would be expressed as being 10¢ over ($5.60 spot − $5.50 futures = $0.10

basis). This immediately tells us that the spot price is greater than the futures price by 10¢.

Of course, the term is not restricted to the difference in price between spot and the nearest futures month. This would be the case only when basis is referred to in general terms, say in a discussion of present market conditions. If our manufacturing jeweller in Amsterdam purchased spot silver at $5.60 and sold September futures at $5.63, his basis would also be said to be 3¢ under. But if the jeweller were to sell the December futures rather than September, his basis would be 16¢ under ($5.60 spot − $5.76 December futures = −$0.16 basis).

Consequently, it would be correct to say that the basis can refer to the relationship between the price of any cash transaction or spot price and any related futures price. Remember that the terms 'cash' and 'physical product' are interchangeable. The cash transaction's price is not necessarily the same as the spot price, as we will see in the following example.

Consider the situation of a silver mine in Mexico. Its production cost for silver is, by way of example, $4.95 per ounce. The spot price is $5.60, which allows the mine to sell silver at a profit of 65¢ per ounce. The price difference between the production cost of the mine and the spot price is not 'basis'; it would be referred to as profit margin. But the mine can use futures to hedge its price risk. If, still using the previous example's figures, the mine sold a September futures, its basis would be 68¢ under ($4.95 cost price − $5.63 September futures = −$0.68 basis). See Table 6.3. If it sold a December futures, its basis would be 81¢ under ($4.95 cost price − $5.76 December futures = −$0.81 basis).

Looking at Table 6.3, we have got to use the mine's cash position as our point of reference in order to express the mine's basis. The spot price is not the relevant price; it is relevant only if the cash position was established at the spot price.

The mine owns the cash silver because it produces it. In market jargon, it would be said that the mine is long cash at a cost of $4.95. That cost establishes the point of reference against which any futures price must be discounted for the purposes of calculating basis. Thus, whenever we wish to determine the basis of a position to be hedged, we first have to establish the price at which the position to be hedged was established.

When the mine hedges its cash position by selling September futures, it is said to be short futures at $5.63. In the business of hedging, the truly relevant information is that the mine established a long hedge with basis 68¢ under. The significance of this jargon will become clear in later chapters.

	Cash market			Futures market			Basis	
Position	Qty	Price	Position	Qty	Price	Amount	Position
Long	100 troy ounces	$4.95	Short	20 fut.	$5.63	$0.68	Under

Table 6.3

The calculation of basis using figures from the silver mine example

Basis is a dynamic concept. The examples involving the Dutch jeweller and the Mexican mine indicated the basis at the time that the futures transactions were done. The spot or cash price at which they purchased or produced the cash silver is fixed because it is a completed matter. However, the futures position that was taken in is still an open position. Therefore, the price fluctuations of the futures contract will change the basis continuously. The next important point is to determine the basis when the futures position is exited, or closed out as it is referred to in the market. One would expect that a change in basis has occurred. It is this change in basis that determines whether there is a profit or a loss on a hedged position.

The importance of a change in basis is now evident. The basis changes by widening or narrowing – it widens when the cash price and the futures price move apart, it narrows when the futures price and the cash price move closer together (*see* Figure 6.3). Now here is an important thought. We discussed the fact that futures prices and the spot price would tend to converge in the delivery month of the futures contract. Another way of saying this is that in the futures delivery month, the basis will narrow. However, as Figure 6.3 shows, there is a continuous widening and narrowing of the basis. The prices will not converge in an ordered fashion. In a normal market, however, as the period to the last day for delivery shortens, the carrying cost becomes progressively less. As the carrying cost lessens, the potential for the widening of the basis lessens accordingly.

The market also talks about a basis being weak or strong. These two terms should not be equated with good and bad. There is no such thing as a good basis or a bad basis. Also, the terms should not be confused with favourable or unfavourable. A strong basis is not more or less favourable than a weak basis. A weak basis is also not more likely to change than a strong basis. The two terms are purely technical and no subtle values should be read into them.

A weak basis is a negative basis – since basis refers to the price of spot to futures, it means when the spot price is under or lower than the futures price. The basis is referred to as weak simply because it is negative. We know that in a normal market, the spot price will be lower than the nearest futures, and nearest futures will be lower than deferred futures. We can therefore confidently state that in a normal market, the basis will be weak. A weak or negative basis that

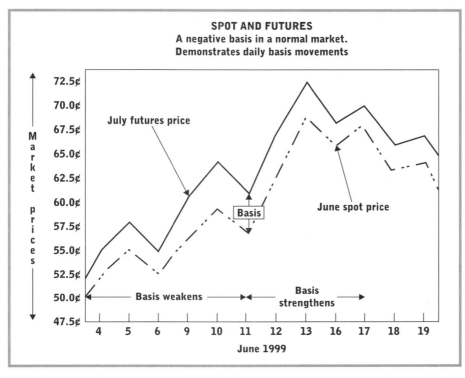

SPOT AND FUTURES
A negative basis in a normal market.
Demonstrates daily basis movements

Figure
6.3

Basis weakens and strengthens continuously

widens is becoming more negative; the basis is weakening. For reasons previously discussed, we know that the basis cannot weaken beyond the carrying cost unless the underlier is a perishable. We know that in the delivery month the basis will narrow. That means it will become less negative, or more positive. We can therefore say that a weak basis will strengthen in the futures delivery month.

A weak basis may, of course, strengthen during the life of the futures contract before delivery. This movement will depend entirely on market forces that influence the price of the underlying commodity and consequently the futures. Indeed, the basis may strengthen to the extent that it changes from a negative basis to a positive basis. Nevertheless, the basis will narrow during the delivery month and will tend to zero.

A positive basis is a strong basis. This is established when the spot price is higher than the futures price. We know that this type of market condition prevails when there is a shortage of the underlying. A strong basis that widens is becoming more positive, or stronger. This means that the spot price is soaring ever higher over the futures price. We know there is no limit to the premium of spot over futures. However, we are well aware that this state of affairs cannot continue. In the futures delivery month the prices will tend to converge.

Therefore, it is a fact that a strong basis will weaken in the futures delivery month.

As in the case of a weak basis that strengthens, a strong basis may weaken long before delivery month. It too can weaken to the extent that an originally positive basis becomes a negative basis. Again, this does not influence the fact that the basis will narrow in the delivery month and tend to zero. In the final analysis, we can state that the basis will narrow in the delivery month, whatever its previous position. If the basis is strong, it will weaken by narrowing, and if it is weak, it will strengthen by narrowing. Either way, the prices must converge for the reasons we have discussed. Table 6.4 illustrates the attributes of basis in futures contracts.

Taking into consideration everything we have said regarding basis, it must be evident that there is quite a lot we can predict about basis movement. We cannot predict its day-to-day movement, which may fluctuate wildly, but we know what the result will be at futures delivery date. We may not know the precise basis that will be reached when the delivery date arrives, but we can predict that the basis will be narrow – it will not be zero, but it will approach zero. The important thing to keep in mind is that within certain reasonably tight parameters, basis is a known and predictable element of futures.

The Risk

As always, our concern as hedgers is with the risk that we incur. From the discussion on basis, we can see that the risk is not linearly connected to the price moves of the underlying commodity. One could say that the price of a futures contract is anticipatory in nature. The price anticipates the price of the underlying at a certain date in the future. Although the spot price must and does influence that expectation, the expectation does not rise and fall penny for penny with the price of the underlying. For this reason, there will be movement in the basis during the course of the contract, right up to delivery date. Nevertheless, apart from basis moves, the price of futures will track the spot price of the underlying.

It follows that a long futures position will gain in value when the price of the underlying commodity rises. The risk of a long futures position, therefore, is that the price of the underlying will fall. Similarly, a short futures position will gain in value if the price of the underlying falls, but will lose if the underlying's price rises. The risk of a short futures position is a rise in the price of the underlying. Although the risk is not linearly connected to the price of the underlying, the risk that is incurred on a futures position is linearly connected to the price of futures (*see* Figure 6.4).

	It is known as a weak basis
Negative basis	The cash price is under the futures price
	It indicates a normal market
	The basis will strengthen by narrowing in the delivery month
Positive basis	It is known as a strong basis
	The cash price is over the futures price
	It indicates an inverse market
	The basis will weaken by narrowing in the delivery month

Table 6.4

The attributes of basis in futures contracts

The fact that the risk is not linearly connected to the price of the underlying will affect the effectiveness of the hedge. This is because the rise or fall in the price of futures will not match the rise or fall in the price of the underlying. The result is that the profit or loss that you make on the futures market will not be equal to the profit or loss that you make on the cash market. This is due to basis moves, which we will discuss when we deal with basis risk. However, as far as the making of a profit or loss in the futures market itself is concerned, the risk is linear.

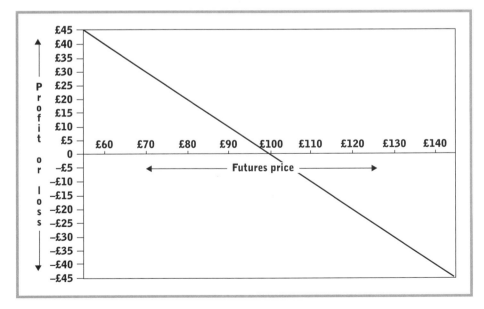

Figure 6.4

The risk profile of a short futures position entered at £100

CHAPTER SEVEN

Options on Futures

Background

Options on futures contracts are a comparatively recent development and their introduction was probably the most important innovation in the futures markets since their founding. They have made the futures markets user friendly and extremely flexible. Armed with the dual instruments of futures and options on futures, businesses are fully equipped to engage in the business of hedging. Not only does this provide flexibility and increased safety, it also allows smaller amounts to be hedged. One of the major drawbacks of the OTC instruments has always been that they are available only in rather large denominations of a million or more. Futures and options on futures largely redress this problem.

The discussion here does not in any way derogate from what we have already said about options. Everything here adds to the principles enunciated earlier. It makes sense that certain changes would be required in order to make an option exchange-tradable. Ordinarily, options can be tailor-made to suit the requirements of the parties. When a standardized agreement, such as a futures contract, becomes the underlying, as is the case with options on futures, it necessitates certain changes. The major adjustments are encapsulated in option standardization and option classification.

Option Standardization

As we have noted, on an exchange there is no room for negotiation on anything other than price. The rest must be a given. Once the exact nature of the article being auctioned is a known fact, the only remaining question is what the market is prepared to offer and bid for that article in terms of money. Of course, there are only two types of options – calls and puts. This is true also for options on futures.

It follows that all the elements of options have to be standardized, except for the premium. You will recall that the price of an option is the premium. So the first standardized element of an option on futures is the futures contract that forms its underlying.

The Underlying Futures Contract

Exchanges offer options on futures contracts that trade on that exchange. In other words, one cannot buy an option on the CBOT on a contract that trades on the London Interest and Financial Futures Exchange (Liffe). This is a situation that is fluid and may change. The co-operative agreement between the Chicago Board of Trade and the Eurex (the derivatives exchange jointly owned by the Swiss Stock Exchange and the Deutsche Borse) in Frankfurt is a taste of what lies ahead. There will be agreements that will result in the products of one exchange becoming tradable on another. The principle remains firm, however. Each exchange offers and takes responsibility for its own contracts. The co-operative agreements merely facilitate trading of futures and options on futures through one exchange to another.

Options usually trade physically on the floor of an exchange in a pit next to the pit where the underlying contract is traded. As a result, one can trade only options offered by an exchange on its contracts. Exchanges do not necessarily offer options on all available contracts. In addition, the ranges of available options differs from contract to contract.

The Option Expiration Date

The next element that is standardized is the option expiration date. A futures contract, say on soybeans, is offered by an exchange for the standard delivery months of March, May, July, September and December. Options on the soybean contract may be offered with expirations that do not coincide with the delivery months. As an example, options might be offered that expire on the third Friday of every calendar month. If this were the case, one would find that an option with expiry on the third Friday of January would have the March soybean futures contract as underlier. The same would apply to the February options. However, the March options would have July futures as underlier.

It is only to be expected that an option with a futures contract as underlier must expire before the underlier ends. If this were not so, there would in fact be no underlier. Keep in mind that if an option expires in the money, the holder is assigned a futures position in the underlying contract. In the case of a call option, the holder will be assigned a long futures, while in the case of a put, a short futures position will be assigned.

For all practical purposes, futures contracts' lives end on the first delivery day. Open contracts are then being executed. If the option expiry date were to coincide or even to post-date the first delivery day of the underlying futures, the option holder would not have any opportunity to offset the assigned futures position. The person may be called upon to take or give delivery of the physical the moment the option expires in the money. This would negate the whole purpose of having options with futures contracts as underlier. Due to these considerations, option expiration dates will always predate the delivery month of the underlying futures contract.

Options are offered with fixed strike prices. The exchange will always specify the strike intervals, depending on the price quote of the underlying futures and the size of the contract.

Taking the CME Swiss franc futures contract as an example, the quote is in US cent per Swiss franc. The options on this contract have strikes every ½¢. You will find strikes on 70¢, on 70.5¢ and again on 71¢, depending on the actual exchange rate that the futures contract is trading on.

Not all the possible strikes can be traded on a particular day. In order to control trading of deep out-of-the-money as well as deep in the money options, the exchange will allow only a certain number of strikes out-of-the-money and in the money to trade. The tradable strikes therefore change as the price of the futures contract changes. However, once there are open option positions on particular strikes, they may be traded, otherwise the parties concerned would be locked into those positions.

These rules will not by themselves impinge on the liquidity of any particular strike. But the movement of the contract price must affect liquidity at every strike. If, for example, the Swiss franc were to trade at 70¢, a speculator might buy a call at strike 71¢ because he believes the franc will rise against the dollar. The strike is out-of-the-money, but only just. Let us assume the franc now experiences a sharp drop to 50¢ – an unlikely event, but just to illustrate the point. The 71¢ call is not going to experience a lot of buyer interest. There will certainly be enough liquidity for the speculator to close out his position, but obviously there will be a lot less interest than there was when the futures rate was at 70¢. This lack of interest is obviously one of the factors that will dramatically reduce the premium. So, the drop in liquidity for that strike is quite understandable. The strikes that bracket the 50¢ mark will obviously enjoy very high liquidity, whether for calls or for puts.

The standardized features allow for a variety of options. As options on futures became increasingly popular, the exchanges initiate many innovative permutations. Thus on many popular contracts there are options with weekly expirations, in addition to options with monthly expirations, while the usual options with expiration closer to the contract delivery month are also available. The trading of options is also becoming more liquid further into the future as their popularity increases, so that longer-term option positions become feasible.

With the standardized elements that we have discussed, options become exchange tradable. These standardized features allow options to be classified and therefore easily identified. Consequently, our next step is to investigate the classification of options.

Option Classification

Options have to be easily identifiable in order to avoid confusion regarding the precise option that is being dealt with at a particular time. Classification solves this problem (*see* Table 7.1). Through option classification it is possible to identify exactly which option is being offered and on which option is being bid in the hurly-burly of the options trading pit.

We already know that there are only two types of option – calls and puts. For the purposes of the second part of the classification as shown in the second column of Table 7.1, one has to mention the type of option as well as its underlying. For example, if one refers to S&P 500 call options, one is referring to a whole class of options. Within that class of options, there are still options with a great variety of strike prices and expiration dates.

It follows that in order to specify a particular option, one needs to give more information. For that reason, it is necessary to name the series of the option. If you wished to purchase a call option on the silver contract that trades on the Comex, you would have to specify the series in order to place your order. The full description in your order to your broker might be to buy five Comex silver March 575 calls. As another example you might tell him to sell three CME Japanese yen April 830 puts.

In the first example, you are telling your broker that the five options you want to buy trade on the Comex. The underlying of the options you want are silver futures contracts, which do in fact trade on the Comex. Remember that the underlying of an option on futures is the relevant futures contract and not the physical commodity.

Next, you are telling your broker that the expiration date of the option must be March. You do not have to specify the year – the broker will assume you wish to trade in the near March option unless you specify differently. Notice that the month does not refer to the delivery date of the futures contract but to the expiration date of the option. The exchange's option specification will prescribe the delivery date of the underlying futures contract. In other words, an option on a silver futures contract, which expires in March, will always have an underlying silver futures contract with a particular, specified delivery month. It is one of the standardized features of an option on futures.

In the second example, you are instructing your broker to sell three put options on the Japanese yen contract that trades on the Chicago Mercantile Exchange. You are also specifying that the

Type of option	Class of option	The option series	
Specifies whether it is a *call* or a *put* option	Indicates all option contracts of the *same type* that cover the *same underlying* futures contract	Refers to all option contracts of the *same class* with the *same strike* price and the *same expiration* date	**Table 7.1**

The classification of options

options must have a strike price of 83¢ to the yen. The broker now knows exactly what it is you want him to do. He can duly take the necessary action to fill your order, except that you have not yet specified the premium at which you wish the transaction to be done. Exactly how orders should be given to brokers fall outside the scope of this book, but this is not a matter to be taken lightly as your instructions to your broker must be correct and unambiguous. Your broker will be happy to supply you with material that sets out the market standard form of instructions which must be used since they are designed to obviate misunderstanding and protect all parties.

Selling Options on Futures

A special word is required on the selling of options on futures exchanges. Just as in the case of futures contracts, you do not have to be the holder of an option in order to sell it. Putting it differently, you can short an option without holding a long option. Obviously, you can short either a put or a call. There are no restrictions on the selling of options on futures exchanges.

The market also uses the term 'writing an option' interchangeably with 'selling an option'. Actually, you 'write' an option when you initiate a position by selling an option. The seller of the option is then referred to as the option writer. When someone writes an option without holding a futures position that would be deliverable against the option if exercised, the person is said to write naked options. Alternatively, it is said that the option is not covered. Writing uncovered or naked options exposes the writer to serious risk of loss.

Writing Naked Options

To illustrate this, consider a trader who writes a call option that moves deep into the money. If it were then exercised, the option holder would receive a long futures position. The writer, or seller, of the option would be assigned a short futures position. The price of the underlying must have risen substantially for the call option to come into the money so deeply that the holder considered it advantageous to exercise. The writer's short futures position will keep on losing money while the price of the underlying rises.

Being short futures in a rising market is clearly an unenviable position, one that everybody would wish to avoid at all costs. Let's keep our discussion on options in a previous chapter in mind. At that time, we illustrated the option writer's risk profile in an illustration. The writer of an option had a limited profit but unlimited risk. The writer of a call option, as in the present example, would face unlimited risk on a rise in the price of the underlying.

Writing Covered Options

The trader in the above example would have been in a much better position had he written a covered call. Consider the example illustrated in Figure 7.1. On January 4, the trader bought five March precious metals futures contracts at 554¢ per ounce. The contract size is 5,000 ounces and the option strikes are spaced every 25¢. The options offered ōn this contract, like most options on futures, are American-style options. The total value of the five contracts is $138,500 (554¢ × 5,000 ounces × 5 contracts), given the price at which the futures were entered. Please note that there is no precious

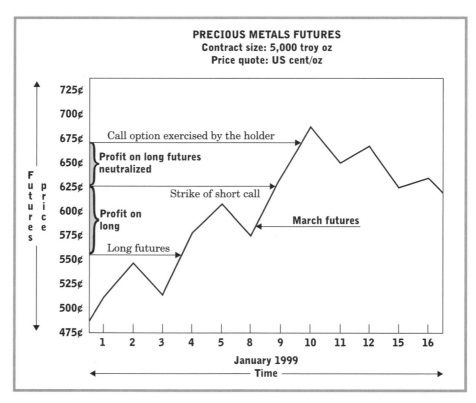

Figure
7.1

The dynamics of a covered write

metals futures contract as such although there are futures contracts on specific precious metals such as gold and silver. This example is used merely to illustrate the principle of a covered write. Each precious metal has its own futures contracts that trade on various exchanges throughout the world.

In our example, the trader took long futures positions because he expected a rise in the price of precious metals. He was certain it would rise by at least 50¢ per ounce to 604¢, giving him a profit of $12,500.00 (50¢ × 5,000 × 5). On the other hand, he was unsure exactly how far the market would rise beyond 604¢. Also, precious metal prices are known to be volatile, so prices could easily retreat again. Of course, if prices retreated before he could close out his futures positions, he would make less on his trade than he anticipated. Depending on the extent of the correction, he could even face a loss if his reaction time was too slow. He therefore had to look at some of the alternatives available to him.

His first possible course of action was merely to take the five long futures at 554¢ while taking no other measures, thereby risking the vagaries of price movement. Preferably, however, he could try to manipulate the situation to give him an advantage. Consequently, he looked at option prices and noticed that the 625¢ call was trading at 17¢. He decided to sell five calls at the same time that he bought the five futures contracts. This strategy gave him an immediate cash advantage of $4,250 (17¢ × 5,000 × 5). The long futures position and the short calls are indicated in Figure 7.1.

We can now examine his position. The five calls he wrote are covered by the five long futures contracts he holds. Because of this situation, he no longer faces unlimited risk on a rise in price. He has also given himself a 'cushion' of $4,250, or putting it differently, he has given himself a margin for error of 17¢ per ounce. When the price of futures rose as he had anticipated (*see* Figure 7.1), he profited all the way until it hit the strike of the short calls at 625¢. When the futures price continued to rise beyond the strike of the calls, the profit on the five long futures was neutralized by the losses incurred on the five short call positions.

Let us consider the situation of the holder of the five calls for a moment. A fund manager bought the five calls as a short-term hedge for a premium of 17¢, paying a total of $4,250. She exercised the options when futures traded at 669¢. When she exercised the five calls, she was assigned five long futures contracts at a price of 625¢. At the same time that she exercised the calls, she put in an order to sell five futures contracts. She sold the five futures at 669¢. Her exercising of the options and the shorting of the futures were virtually simultaneous. She was therefore long five futures at 625¢ and short five at 669¢. Her gross profit was therefore 44¢ per ounce. Against this gross profit, she had incurred a cost of 17¢ per ounce.

Her net profit, excluding commissions, was consequently 27¢ per ounce or $6,750 on the deal. That would not be too shabby a return on an investment of $4,250.

Our trader friend did not do badly either. When the calls were exercised, he was assigned five short futures at 625¢, being the strike of his short calls. The five long futures that covered the five short calls were immediately closed out by the assignment of the five short futures. He was long at 554¢ and now short at 625¢, leaving him a profit of 71¢ per ounce. He was out of the futures market with a total profit of $17,750 (71¢ profit × 5,000 ounces × 5 contracts).

Now he does not have any futures position. Of course, the five call options were destroyed by being exercised. However, in addition to the profit he netted on the futures, he still has the premium of $4,250 that he collected when he sold the five calls. For his trouble, he took home a net profit of $22,000.

If we compare the outcome of the trader's covered call trade to the outcome that the uncovered call would have left him with, it is apparent that he has benefited greatly by the covered write.

This simple example illustrates the danger of writing naked options against the advantages of writing covered ones.

CHAPTER EIGHT

Derivatives Risk

The purpose of this chapter is to create awareness that, apart from the intentional risk that you incur when dealing in derivatives, there are other, unwanted risks. In previous chapters we have alluded to some of these risks. A slightly different perspective is required from the one normally found in books dealing with the subject. This book is intended for people involved in business and not specifically for the banking industry, therefore it requires a different perspective. Most companies will be able to avoid these risks by leaving them to the banks, which are well able to deal with them.

Those involved in the world of banking have to comply with stringent controls and the regulation of capital adequacy. Taking financial risk is their business. Therefore, it is imperative that they measure and keep track of the exact nature, size and implications of every transaction. The risks are no less real for the ordinary business. Apart from what was said about leaving the banks to handle your derivatives risk, there is a further difference. The financial risk portfolio of a business firm would usually not be as large or as complex as that of a bank or other financial institution. For that very reason, businesses outside of finance and banking, risk taking through derivatives and other financial instruments should be restricted to the purposes of hedging

Of course, there are firms that are so enormous and have such large international exposure to interest rates, currencies and commodity price risk that their hedging activities become as great and sometimes even greater than the activities of some banks. An example is General Electric (GE) which, together with their subsidiary General Electric Capital Services, is one of the largest users of derivatives outside the financial and banking services. In its 1995 annual report, the company's policy on financial instruments is clearly stated. It makes use of various financial instruments to manage its interest rate and currency risk. However, it does not engage in market making, trading or any speculative activities in the derivatives markets.

There is a lesson for every business firm in GE's policy. First, it is very active in hedging and otherwise managing its risks. Second, in that activity it makes extensive use of derivatives. Third, when it comes to taking risk, it sticks to its core business. Derivatives are used solely to hedge and manage the unwanted risks that are both unavoidable and incidental to the core business. This sound policy deserves the compliment of imitation by all other businesses.

As we have said, there are some unwanted and unavoidable risks associated with derivatives. These must be assessed and minimized. They are not risks that should preclude a company from dealing in derivatives. The purpose here is to make the reader aware of the risks and to caution the choice of counter parties, agents, etc.

Basis Risk

Basis risk is the risk that the price of the underlying of a derivative will not track the price of the derivative perfectly. We discussed this phenomenon at length in Chapter 6. When we deal with hedging by using futures and options, we will deal with the movement of basis again as it is a very important element that has to be taken into account at all times.

Basis risk is really only a factor in futures hedging. None of the other derivatives presents us with the problem of basis. There are a number of reasons why a hedge with a moveable basis may be imperfect (*see* Table 8.1). It is also important to note that basis risk is a double-edged sword – it can result in a loss or a profit on a hedge.

Examining these reasons, we may note that the first reason was fully discussed in Chapter 6. Price disparities occur as a result of the widening or narrowing of the basis. However, these moves occur within reasonably predictable parameters, and techniques in fact allow us to take advantage of the known movement of basis.

Grade disparities occur where the hedger is not hedging the actual grade of the commodity that is reflected in the futures price. This often happens in agricultural commodities, where a specific grade of, say, wheat is the basis grade of the futures. The farmer, who wishes to hedge the price for his crop, may reap a lower grade. The price of the lower grade of wheat may not have risen as high, or fallen as low, as the price of the basis grade. The effect is that his futures position may have moved more or less as much as the price of the wheat he has hedged. This disparity will influence the effectiveness of the hedge, but will not negate it. In fact, it may result in an additional profit, depending on the direction of the relative price moves. This will be discussed fully later. The problem faced by the farmer is also faced by the interest rate hedger using Treasury bond futures. If one holds US Treasury bills and you wish to hedge their value with futures contracts, the nominal bills that undertake the futures contract will probably not correspond exactly to the bills you hold. This presents virtually the same problem as a grade discrepancy because the price sensitivity of the bonds you hold will not be equal to the sensitivity of the futures. There are, however, ways of calculating equivalencies that address these problems.

Prices disparities	Futures prices and spot prices may change in the same direction, but not in the same amount
Grade disparities	The price of the basis grade of the futures may not be tracked directly by price changes in other grades
Lot size disparities	Futures contracts are sized in round lots and may not equal the quantity hedged
Product disparities	Price changes in primary products may not equal price changes in secondary products

Table 8.1

Reasons why a hedge with a moveable basis may be imperfect

Lot size disparities exist because of the standard contract sizes of futures. It may be that the contract size for a metal is 1,000 ounces and the hedger holds 4,550 ounces. The first option is to hedge by using four futures contracts. In that case 550 ounces of the metal will not be hedged and will still be subject to adverse price fluctuation. The second alternative is to five futures contracts. The futures position will exceed the cash position by 450 ounces. The 450 ounces futures position will not be covered by any cash holding, so the risk of an adverse price change in the futures will have to be faced. In neither case will the hedge be perfect. However, this disadvantage is slight in view of the fact that the greater part of this cash holding can be hedged.

Product disparities arise where the hedger is unable to hedge his cash holding directly because of the unavailability of a futures contract for that particular product. This situation is prevalent in so-called 'secondary' product hedging. Futures contracts tend to be available for primary products, such as base and precious metals, crude oil, gas and agricultural produce. There are futures contracts for copper metal, but not for secondary copper products such as copper cable and copper pipes. It is standard practice to hedge positions in secondary products by taking futures positions in primary products. You will appreciate, though, that changes in the price of copper will not be reflected exactly by changes in the price of copper cable. Although the price of copper may be the single largest factor in determining the price of copper cable, there are other factors of production, supply and demand that influence the price of copper cable. This disparity will be responsible for inefficiencies in such a hedge, but the hedge will still be vastly superior to a totally unhedged position.

Hedging with futures is often described as a process whereby direct price risk is exchanged for basis risk. Basis risk is a risk that is quantitatively smaller and with much lower volatility, and is thus much less risky than direct price risk. Also, as we have seen, there are certain basic predictions that we can make about the movement of basis which we are unable to make with as much certainty about the prices of commodities.

Credit Risk

Credit risk in derivatives is the risk that a counterparty will fail to meet its obligations. The credit risk in exchange-traded derivatives has been dealt with extensively. The conclusion was that the credit risk in dealing with an exchange and its clearinghouse is negligible. The same may not be true of the broker that you work through. Generally, in developed nations, the futures markets are strictly regulated, controlled and insured. Therefore, even the risk of dealing with brokers may be limited. The major issue is really that you should have a broker that you trust and that you are comfortable with to do business.

Over-the-counter instruments are a different matter altogether. In OTCs the risk is directly between the parties. You should only enter into swaps and OTC options with counterparties whose credit rating is up to the standard that you require. Keep in mind that the impact of credit risk to off-balance sheet derivatives is not the same as to cash instruments. In the case of cash instruments, credit risk imperils the principal. This is also true of the impact of credit risk on currency swaps because the principal is in fact delivered at maturation. The case of interest rate swaps is different. In interest rate swaps, there is only notional principal – principal actually never changes hands, therefore only interest is threatened.

Banks often use default risk as a measure to express risk on interest rate swaps. Whereas credit risk measures the probability of default, default risk measures the probable loss due to default. Some prefer to use this measure because it is only loss of interest that is at risk on an interest rate swap. The size of the loss therefore depends on how interest rates move during the currency of the swap.

Default risk is often quantified in terms of replacement cost. Institutions usually assume that swap counterparties will immediately try to replace a defaulting counterparty to a swap. For the purposes of the valuation, it is assumed that a replacement swap will not represent much of a disturbance to the floating rate-based stream of income. They largely ignore that stream, as it is reset periodically in any event. The valuation is therefore rather based on the disturbance default will cause to the fixed-income stream. This may be negligible, but it could also be substantial. A mismatch of reset dates can also have serious cost implications.

The impact of credit risk can be minimized in various ways, the two most important being through netting and taking collateral. It is estimated that by a combination of netting and collateral, total credit risk can be halved. The taking of collateral also involves risk – that the value of the collateral may diminish during the term of the derivative. This can quite easily be provided for by requiring a top up of collateral whenever necessary.

However, most businesses should not have too much difficulty with credit risk. If you limit your dealings in OTC derivatives to Standard and Poor's AAA or AA-rated banks, the credit risk that you face in your business should be negligible. You can also spread the risk by dealing with a number of banks, although that would be necessary only if the nominal capital of your derivative transactions runs into tens of millions of dollars.

For energy swaps, most firms should be adequately protected if they do business only with the large international oil companies. Again, you are not restricted to doing business with just one company. Even if you purchase your energy requirements through contract or franchise with one particular oil company, you should not have any difficulty in doing oil-related swaps with any of the other companies.

For the sake of clarity, ease of use and for the minimum number of administrative complications, always try to structure swaps so that the two cash flows' payments coincide and netting takes place. Not only should the netting of the two payments in one swap be provided for, but when the number of swaps with one party starts accumulating, make sure that all payments on all transactions with the same counterpart are netted. This will not only ease the burden, it will, by itself, reduce credit risk.

The above observations also apply to options. The option writer faces the real risk; the option-buying counterparty has no further price risk once the premium has been paid. However, if you are the buyer, the ability of the option writer to perform his obligation when you exercise the option is of concern to you. Once again, if AAA or AA-rated banks were the option writers, most firms would be comfortable. If your firm is the writer, your credit rating will come into the calculation of the counterparty. You will, however, not face any credit risk from the counterparty once it has paid the premium.

Legal Risk

Legal risk is applicable only when dealing in OTCs. The only agreement required for trading on futures exchanges is a proper agreement between yourself and your broker. Trading on an exchange automatically binds all parties to the terms and conditions of the contract as prescribed by the exchange.

Although banks and financial institutions are usually awash with legal documentation, companies often neglect this aspect of risk. Legal risk is the risk of legal unenforceability of agreements, especially when international cross-border agreements are drafted. There are a number of aspects that one should ensure through competent legal opinion.

The first concern should be that the people acting on behalf of the counterparty have the necessary legal authority to act on behalf of and to bind the counterparty. The second concern should be that the documentation is sufficient and that all the terms and conditions have been properly described. Before any action is taken in terms of any agreement, the integrity of the documentation should be thoroughly established.

When dealing with foreign counterparties or counterparties that operate from foreign countries, it is advisable to agree on the legal system that will govern the interpretation and application of the agreement. Leaving the governing law of the contract to sort itself out according to the tenets of private international law can be an exciting adventure. You will get to meet world-famous lawyers, visit strange countries with even stranger legal systems, while all the time getting the opportunity to pay breathtakingly exorbitant legal fees.

One of the best ways to avoid these pitfalls is to use a properly rated indigenous bank as counterparty or as guarantor. If this is not possible, make sure that the documentation used is the market-standard master agreement, such as those provided by the International Swaps and Derivatives Association, or the British Bankers' Association.

If your company's derivatives transactions are numerous, it is advisable to have a legal audit done at least annually. The in-house legal department can undertake this job or it can be outsourced to legal firms that specialize in derivatives.

Operational Risk

Unexpected losses can arise from derivatives through deficiencies in your information systems and internal controls. You have to make sure that your firm has in place a comprehensive system for capturing and monitoring derivatives risk before you embark on their use in any volume.

This risk can be avoided only if you have a proper system whereby every derivative transaction is fully recorded and where the system will remind you of important upcoming dates. Imagine that you have a long futures position on Brent crude, and you neglect to offset the position before delivery date. One morning when you arrive at the office, you are liable to find a few thousand barrels of oil sitting on your doorstep.

The message of this section is merely to get you to arrange your internal systems in such a fashion that your way of handling derivatives does not by itself create risk of loss. It is imperative that you keep proper track and control of every derivatives position. Only then will you be able to realize the full advantages that they offer you in your business.

PART THREE

The Business
of Hedging

CHAPTER NINE

Laying the groundwork

Background

Before you can undertake the hedging of risk in your business, there is some groundwork to be done. A lot of it is reasonably obvious, but there are some pitfalls to watch out for. It is better to spend time doing the preparatory work properly, than to rush into action only to find that the results are neither what you expected nor what you required.

The methodology in this book is to consistently explain the principles involved in every element of the subject matter. This is founded on the belief that once a principle is understood, it is easier to identify and deal with the specifics by applying the principle. So it is in this chapter and in those that follow. The point is that nobody knows and understands your business as well as you do. By explaining the principles involved in hedging and by illustrating them through practical examples, you will be able to identify and deal with similar issues in your own business.

It is impossible in a work such as this to cover the many permutations of risks that arise or might apply to specific businesses. It is up to you to go through your business to discover through analysis exactly what the risks are that you face. Then you must decide how best to deal with them. Use the information in this and the following chapters to help you. They do not contain recipes to be slavishly followed. Rather, they contain ideas and clues that can lead you to better manage risk in your business.

Analyzing the Risk

Before any hedging strategy can be decided upon or implemented, it is essential to analyze the risk that you need to hedge. Keep in mind that the purpose of the analysis is to determine the most appropriate hedging instrument and hedging strategy. We already know that in order to achieve this, you have to take on a risk that is equal and opposite to the risk that you want to hedge. The questions that the analysis should deal with are set out in Table 9.1.

Directionality	Is the risk related to a price move downwards or upwards?
The quantitative risk	What is the amount of principal involved?
Risk duration	Over what period is the principal at risk?
Risk periodicity	Are there rollovers or periodic cash flows during the exposure period?
The risk index	To what index is the risk linked?

Table 9.1

The factors that need to be determined by an analysis of risk

Determining Risk Directionality

The question of directionality posed in 9.1 is self-explanatory and also seemingly simple to answer. In our discussion on the three risks of the apocalypse – the price of money, the price of commodities, and systemic risk – we stated that interest rates reflect the cost of domestic currency, while exchange rates reflect the cost of domestic currency relative to another currency. Both rates influence the cost of money to an enterprise and ultimately, therefore, its profitability.

The directionality of the risk faced by a borrower of money will be upwards while an investor's risk directionality will be downwards.

Consider a business that owes foreign currency, or is required to make payment in future in a foreign currency. That business faces a fall of the domestic currency against the foreign currency. The domestic currency's fall in relative value will increase the cost to the business since more of the domestic currency will be required to make the payment. The directionality of the risk in domestic currency is therefore downwards, but upwards in the foreign currency. In foreign currency, the risk directionality changes with the perspective from which it is viewed.

Against that, a business holding foreign currency or expecting to receive foreign currency faces downward risk in the foreign currency and upward risk in the domestic currency. An upward move of the domestic currency will translate into less domestic currency being received from the foreign currency held or received.

Similarly, in commodities, the person who is long a commodity faces the risk of a fall in price because that will devalue his holding. A person who is short the commodity will risk a rise in price because that will oblige him to pay a higher price for the commodity when he needs to purchase it.

Systemic risk may appear to be more involved, but it is identical to the commodity situation. Remember that systemic risk is created by those factors at large in the world economy, the domestic economy, or a particular industry that may influence the performance of businesses that operate within the system. These factors may have a positive or a negative influence on business performance. In other words, the risk directionality, as in all other instances, may be either upwards or downwards.

It follows that a person who is long stocks or equities faces the risk of a downturn, while those who are short stocks and equities face upward risk directionality.

Determining the Quantitative Risk

This is simply the amount of principal at risk. It is the principal amount borrowed or invested. In a foreign currency deal, it is the present value in the domestic currency of the amount of foreign currency involved.

A slightly different problem is presented by a floating rate loan where periodic repayments include capital and interest. Since the amount of principal would diminish after every repayment, it might be advisable to regard each period between instalments as a separate loan for the principal outstanding. The same would apply, *mutatis mutandis*, to an investment or loan that was repaid through periodic instalments that included capital and interest.

The quantitative risk in commodities is the spot price per unit of the commodity times the number of units to be hedged, or alternatively, the actual cost at which the hedger acquired the relevant quantity of the cash commodity. For a short cash position, the quantitative risk would be equal to the selling price per unit of the commodity times the number of units of the commodity.

Quantitative systemic risk may be more problematic. As we have said, holding stock in a company exposes the holder to individual stock risk as well as to systemic risk. A business or company as a whole is neither more nor less than a basket of risks. One cannot hedge the performance of an individual stock unless there is a stock option available on that particular stock. If one were an investor in stock, individual stock risk could be considerably dampened through portfolio diversification until virtually only systemic risk remained.

A company or person holding an equity portfolio must have the risk profile and the VAR of that particular portfolio determined. That value will then constitute the principal or quantitative risk.

Much the same considerations will apply if you wished to hedge the value of your own company or business. You could only hedge that value against systemic risk. You would need to determine the value at risk as if for a portfolio in order to determine the quantitative risk. The quantitative risk is important because it obviously determines the quantitative measure of the hedging risk.

Risk Duration

Normally, it is quite simple to determine the period for which the principal would be at risk. However, the period is not always obvious. Consider the case where an investment is made at a fixed interest rate for three months. This type of investment is technically not at risk to variations in interest rates. However, if it is the intention to reinvest the amount after each period of three months, the reinvestment is at risk of a decline in interest rates – on the reinvestment date, you might get a lower rate of interest than the rate at which it is presently invested.

Analyzing the example, the quantitative measure would be the capital to be reinvested and the risk duration would be three months. This situation could also be approached as a problem of periodicity if the reinvestments were to continue for a definite period (*see* below). The difference in approach would influence the hedging instrument selected or the way it was constructed in order to hedge the risk.

The same considerations will apply to a term loan at a fixed interest rate. If the intention were to roll over the loan after every term, the rollover would be at risk of rising interest rates. If the rollovers were intended to continue for a fixed period, the intended period would be regarded as the duration, while the rollover periods would be regarded as periodicity.

In the case of commodities, a number of other considerations would be relevant. If a commodity is to be held for a period before it is used or resold, that period is the risk period. However, if a commodity has been sold forward with the intention of buying it in at a particular time, the risk period is the period between the time it was sold and the intended time for buying it in. There are many other examples, but the astute businessperson will realize when he is at risk of a rise or a fall in price of a commodity.

In the case of a portfolio, duration is calculated by weighting certain factors in the basket of risks to adjust for individual durations.

Risk Periodicity

This element is related to the previous one. The task here is to determine how often, during the total duration of the risk, the price or rate is subject to adjustment. Consider the example of a two-year loan with interest rate adjustments made quarterly. The duration is obviously two years and the periodicity of the risk is quarterly. Similarly, a loan over three years at a floating interest rate with monthly instalments would have risk duration of three years and risk periodicity of one month.

Now consider the example of an order for foreign manufactured goods. Assume that the goods are ordered at a fixed price to be paid in a foreign currency. The ordered goods will be delivered over a period of two years. Delivery will be made every three months and payment for each batch is to be effected against delivery by letter of credit. Risk duration is two years and risk periodicity is quarterly.

This latter example, slightly modified, can be extended to illustrate periodicity in commodity price risk. Assume that the order is not for a fixed price over a period of two years but at a floating price. The price float could be linked to any number of indexes, e.g. any interest rate index, base metal price index, energy index or any variety of raw material prices. In this example, there would be simultaneous currency risk and commodity price risk. The risk period and the risk periodicity for each risk would be identical, namely two years and quarterly respectively.

Systemic risk periodicity will usually, but not necessarily, coincide with the risk period. Obviously, as long as you hold a particular stock or own a particular business, you are exposed to any systemic risk that the business may be subject to. However, it may not be practical to hedge this risk on a continuous basis. Nevertheless, there are hedging techniques available that may be appropriate to your situation. In this part of the book we will discuss some of these techniques.

The Risk Index

This simply refers to the main factor that influences the price move. It is the underlying factor in the market risk of the relevant instrument or commodity. For example, a loan that is fixed to one or other of the Libor indices is subject to adjustment in terms of the movement of that index. That Libor index is thus the risk index for that loan.

The 'risk index' is actually a misnomer because the factor is not always strictly speaking an index as in the example. The spot price of the cash is usually the origin of the risk. An adverse move in the spot price of gold will impact negatively on the value of your gold mine. In this latter case, the spot price of gold is the risk index of the value of your gold mine because its movement will revalue the gold reserves of the mine upwards or downwards. Its movement will also determine the value of the production of the mine and it will obviously have an influence on profitability.

Selecting the Right Hedging Tool

Armed with the result of the analysis, you are now in a position to select the most appropriate hedging tool. You have at your disposal the whole tool chest that we discussed previously. However, you will find that a number of tools can be used for any one hedge. There is not necessarily a single, objectively viewed, 'best' tool. A lot will depend on your, or the management's, particular criteria for hedging. Let us look at the factors that should generally influence your choice.

Meeting the Risk Criteria

The first criteria that must be taken into account are the parameters set by your risk analysis. Obviously, the closer the hedging tool comes to meeting all of the criteria, the better it will perform as a hedge. Any business will have certain limitations to what it can do and these may impact heavily on your choice of instruments. But your first priority must be to establish as perfect a hedge as possible, given all the circumstances.

The ideal instrument will have the characteristics set out in Table 9.2. You must accept that it will not always be possible to find an instrument that measures up to the risk in the exact manner illustrated by the table.

The Underlier

To illustrate this point it is worth looking at a few examples. First, there may not be a derivative instrument available that has exactly the same underlier as the instrument or commodity price that you want to hedge. This may be especially so if you want to hedge the price of a secondary product. You may need to hedge your investment in flour, but the available derivatives have only wheat as underlier.

Standard Contract Size

Second, you may be unable to obtain an instrument for the exact quantity of the underlier that you need to hedge. This may be the case if you wish to use exchange-traded derivatives with their standard contract sizes, but there may be no swaps or OTC options available for the product you wish to hedge.

Risk Convexity

Third, the risk index may not be identical to the risk index you are exposed to. This may again be because of the fact that you are forced to hedge a secondary product with an instrument with a primary commodity as its underlier. Another reason might be that the risk index of the derivative is not linearly connected to the risk index of the underlier. This would be the case when hedging with futures, where basis movement has to be taken account of.

The risk	The hedge
The risk-originating instrument or commodity	An identical underlier
Risk directionality	Opposite risk directionality
Principal at risk	Quantitatively equal
Duration	Equal duration
Periodicity	Identical periodicity
Risk index	Identical risk index

Table 9.2

The perfect hedge

Developing Guidelines

These, then, are some of the factors you will face in the business of hedging. They all require careful consideration. The advantages of every derivative instrument have to be weighed against its disadvantages. What may be a perfect instrument under one set of conditions may not be perfect under another. It would be wrong therefore, to devise an inflexible hedging policy in a company.

Developing guidelines for a company's hedging policy is entirely a different matter. They are essential because there are other factors that may influence your choice or range of derivatives to be used in your business. The manner of the use of derivatives should also be laid down. The latter refers to the sound policy that derivatives should be used only for hedging, not for assuming 'naked' risk, speculatively. These matters actually pertain to risk management as such and thus fall outside the scope of this book.

We will now move on to investigate some of the other business factors that may influence your choice of derivatives.

Meeting Your Business Criteria

Every business has its own set of circumstances that may broaden or narrow the scope of derivatives that are available to it. It is important, indeed unavoidable, that your hedging policy and the instruments used to that end meet the criteria that best suits your business considerations and environment. Table 9.3 sets out some of the considerations that might influence a business in determining its policy on the use of derivatives.

Risk Aversion

Risk aversion must play a major role in a company's policy on choice of derivatives. It is generally accepted that options have the least

Business considerations	Possible selection criteria
Risk aversion	Only use options or other instruments in conjunction with options. Avoid counterparty credit risk
Limited capital resources	Avoid instruments requiring margin or premium, such as futures and options
Restrictive credit rating	Avoid instruments and positions requiring a credit rating, such as OTC derivatives and short options
Hedge only to protect values or cost	Use only 'straight' derivatives avoiding complicated structures
Exploit windfall profit opportunities	Use options, synthetic positions and some advanced hedging techniques

Table 9.3

Business considerations and the criteria for derivatives choice

risk of all derivatives. A company with high risk aversion should therefore make hedging through the use of options its first choice.

If your company is highly risk averse, keep in mind that the nearer the money is to the strike price of the option, the greater the premium. The premium is at risk, so the higher the premium, the higher the risk. Also, the further out of the money and thus the cheaper the option, the more the price you are trying to hedge can move adversely without the option giving you any protection. The benefit is, of course, that the risk is known and controlled. It can thus be budgeted for. In fact, it can be accommodated as part of the company's cost structure.

Exchange-traded options have the lowest risk. OTC options still have counterparty credit risk, since the option holder must be satisfied that the option writer will be able to perform its side of the bargain. This does not exclude OTC options, but it does mean that the company must scrutinize the counterparty very carefully before striking a deal.

Swaps can still be included in the portfolio of derivatives. The risk is again that of counterparty creditworthiness. Futures may be used only if there is reasonable certainty that basis movement will be in the hedger's favour.

Capital Resources

A company may be reluctant to allocate too much of its capital resources for the purposes of hedging. Futures always do, and some swap counterparties sometimes may require a margin deposit. Options require a premium to be paid. You cannot have the protection of hedging at no cost. So however limited, some capital resources will have to be diverted to hedging. The benefits that accrue will outstrip the cost or inconvenience of the diversion by many leagues. This is a calculation that you will have to make and satisfy yourself on. However, if resources are limited, the company would be well advised to investigate the use of swaps as its first hedging option.

Credit Rating

A firm's credit rating or its high use of the credit facilities presently available to it may restrict its choice in derivative instruments. Futures and options require no credit rating. This is true for options on futures as well as OTC options. These instruments must consequently be such a firm's first choice. These instruments are all off-balance sheet, so they will not influence the firm's credit rating or use more of its credit resources in any way.

Hedging only for Protection

The whole purpose of hedging is, of course, to protect. It can protect the value of assets or of inventory held, or it can lock in the price of assets or inventory to be purchased. In that sense, its aim is to keep costs and values constant. Using hedging for this purpose is the simplest and probably the cheapest way of going about it. The process will use the least resources in terms of time, personnel and trading costs.

By its very nature though, to hedge is to equalize price movement. A simple hedge will keep the cost or value of whatever is being hedged constant. In other words, a straightforward hedge will neutralize adverse price movement, but at the same time it will neutralize any favourable price movement. A company will have to increase its cost of hedging and the trouble that it goes to in the process, if it is to avoid this effect.

For that reason, many companies are quite content with straightforward hedging instruments and techniques. They will enter coupon swaps, take appropriate futures positions, and not bother about all the other permutations and possibilities. Options are not totally avoided, but they involve capital outlays that many companies eschew. If straightforward hedging for its intended purpose meets your business needs, keep it simple. Use swaps and futures.

Windfall Profits

Some companies prefer to exploit whatever windfall opportunities come their way. This attitude prohibits using simple hedging instruments. Of course, options give you the opportunity of hedging against adverse price movement, while retaining some profit potential. The profit potential is however, curtailed by two elements – the premium and by how far the option is OTM.

The breakeven point for an option requires a favourable move of the underlying's price to an amount equal to the premium paid. If the option is bought at the money, any move in a favourable direction will offset the premium paid to a greater or lesser extent. So any favourable move has a salutary effect. However, using certain combinations of swaps and options or futures and options can lead to even better results. There are also techniques for enhancing upside and downside profitability, without abandoning the basic purpose, namely the elimination of risk.

Am I saying that you can make profits without the concomitant of risk? No, I'm not. What I am saying is that you can hedge your business risk without hedging away all profit in the event of a favourable price move. The risk involved will be the cost of doing it, like the cost of an option eats away at the effectiveness of a straight hedge. Yet the profits that can be made are substantial and may be worthwhile if you are a windfall profiteer.

The cost of ensuring maximum profit potential may include premium, additional trading costs, the cost of time spent on monitoring the markets and possibly the cost of additional personnel resources used in the process. Again, it is a calculation you are going to have to make for yourself in your business. Then you will be able to take the decision based on your preferences and requirements.

CHAPTER **TEN**

Hedging the Price of Money

Background

In this chapter we are concerned with the risk inherent in the price of money. Although the examples will therefore specifically deal with this risk, be sure to compare them to the examples in the following chapters. It may be more important for you to recognize the commonality of the examples than to be blinkered by their specifics.

There are a few reasons why a whole chapter is devoted to hedging the price of money. Apart from the fact that it is the one risk that is faced by every business, the foremost reason is that there are special features that apply only to this subject. As you will see during this chapter, a few additional elements should be considered when analysing a business for this type of risk. More importantly, there are special features that apply to the derivatives used for hedging the price of money. These do not negate the universal features of the instruments that we have already considered; rather, they are special adaptations and subtle adjustments to the derivative instruments that arise from the nature of the subject itself.

A further reason for such a long devoted chapter is that it contains the first full-scale working examples of hedging. Notwithstanding the adaptations and subtle adjustments to the instruments used that we have already seen, the examples that follow demonstrate virtually all the universal features of hedging. As you will learn from examples in Chapter 11, the principles of hedging with a particular derivative instrument do not vary greatly from one type of risk to the next. When you understand the mechanics of a particular derivative and you understand the principle of hedging, you can hedge any risk you come across.

A short explanation of how we intend to deal with the subject matter of this chapter is thus required. As we have said, the price of money affects us either because we owe money or because we hold money. First, we can owe money because we have borrowed it or because we entered into a transaction that obliges us to make some payment in the future, either in our home currency or in a foreign currency. Moneys owed should therefore be understood in this broad sense. For ease of reference, I will refer to all moneys owed in this way as borrowings.

Similarly, we can be said to hold money when we have invested money or when, by some transaction, we now possess or will in the future receive foreign currency. The latter is obviously an 'investment' in foreign currency. Again, for ease of reference I will refer to all moneys held in this way as investments.

However, in the context of this chapter, we are concerned only with borrowings that are interest bearing or are due in a foreign currency. Similarly, we are concerned only with investments that bear interest or holdings that are denominated in a foreign currency.

Analyzing Money Price Risk – Additional Factors

In Chapter 9 we established the questions to which we seek answers through our analysis. When you analyze your business to determine the exact nature and extent of your risk to the price of money, you may encounter a number of complicating factors. Before I deal with these, however, let me deal with those factors that are peculiar to risks that pertain to the price of money.

When we attempt to analyze these risks, we must first distinguish between purely interest rate risk and purely currency risk. In Chapter 9 we dealt with the directional and other elements to be determined for the purposes of hedging. These are straightforward when we deal with a single borrowing or investment transaction. We will know immediately what the risk directionality, the principal, the duration, the periodicity and risk index for that transaction are.

However, the analysis may be complicated by a number of factors. A firm may risk a rise in respect of certain transactions while at the same time risking a fall in respect of other transactions. If the risk is linked to the same index, they might partly or completely hedge one another. If the underlying interest rate or currency rate is not identical, they will not hedge one another, although the overall risk may be dampened due to diversification. One might then treat each transaction separately for hedging it. This is not only feasible, it is also the simplest solution, on condition that each transaction is large enough to meet minimum principal requirements of the applicable derivative. Also, keep in mind the cumulative effect of the transaction costs if there are many transactions to be hedged. On condition that each transaction is large enough, transaction costs would be minimal compared with the risk being hedged.

If treating each transaction individually is not realistic in your company's case, the next option would be to net all transactions. Of course, you could not just lump domestic currency interest rate risks together with foreign currency risks. Not even all interest rate risks can necessarily be taken together. The risk profiles of individual transactions may vary substantially. If your company faces such a multiplicity of interest rate and/or exchange rate risks, it would be better to treat these as a risk portfolio. Then you should call in the experts to do this analysis. Your auditors or bank should be able to help if you lack the in-house expertise.

Interest-bearing investments present similar problems. If you hold government paper such as Treasury bonds, bills, notes, or company bonds, you will probably have to determine their equivalency with the risk elements of the hedging instrument. This is done quite easily. There are appropriate formulae available to calculate all such equivalencies. Again, it is better to call in the experts to do the analysis for you. That will place you in a much better position to make use of the best and most appropriate hedging instrument.

Using Swaps

Having dealt with the principles and mechanics of swaps, we can now consider how they are used to hedge risk in the real world. We will illustrate their use by means of various examples, although these do not pretend to be either comprehensive or exhaustive. However, they are intended to adequately demonstrate the use and potential of swaps, to such an extent that you will be able to employ them in your business for hedging away your risk.

The examples that follow demonstrate the simplest and most often used swaps. These are the ones you are most likely to find useful in your business. Because the principles are consistent throughout, you will readily be able to take what is presented here and adapt it to your needs.

One final word before we plunge into the examples. Since swaps are by definition exchanges of income streams, it follows that they are particularly suited to hedge risks that involve possible changes in the value of cash flows. The examples will demonstrate this very clearly. Indeed, it would be extremely inappropriate to use swaps as a hedging tool if the hedged risk did not involve streams of income.

Hedging a bank loan with a coupon swap

Case Study 10.1

In Chapter 4, we met Paula McDermott and Champignon Trust. Paula had been introduced to the trust through her bank of which the trust was also a client. The bank was therefore in a position to assure Paula of the trust's creditworthiness.

Paula approached the bank to arrange a swap after she had obtained a loan from it of $50 million to enable her to improve the research and development facility at her laboratories as well as to

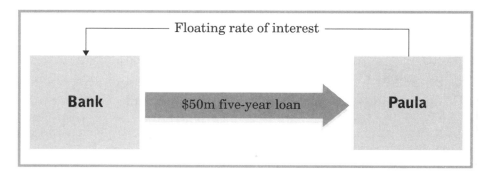

Figure
10.1

The agreement between Paula and her bank

increase her manufacturing capacity. The loan was for a period of five years with interest being paid every six months in arrears. The interest rate was agreed as the dollar six-month Libor rate as at the start of each six-month period (*see* Figure 10.1).

Analyzing the Risk

If we analyze the risk that Paula faces as a result of the bank loan, it is immediately obvious that the directionality of the risk is upwards. Quantitatively the risk is $50 million and the period is five years. The risk periodicity is six months and the risk index is US$ six-month Libor.

Hedging the Risk

As you will recall from the previous chapter, the deal between Paula and Champignon Trust was that Paula would pay a fixed interest rate to the trust, based on a notional principal of $50 million. The trust in turn would pay her floating interest calculated on the same notional principal, based on the six-month US$ Libor. Interest is fixed in advance and paid in arrears. The interest on the bank loan is calculated in the same way.

In the result, Paula faces a directionally downward interest rate risk on the swap. The quantitative risks of the swap and the loan are identical, as are the periods, the periodicities and the risk indexes. The structure of the total hedge is illustrated in Figure 10.2.

Evaluating the Hedge

Now we can investigate how good the hedge is. Paula pays six-month Libor to the bank on account of her loan. She also receives the six-month Libor from the trust. When Paula structured the deal, she ensured that the periodicity of the hedge and the loan were the same. She also ensured that the date of payment, and therefore the fixing date of Libor for the swap, was for the payment and fixing of

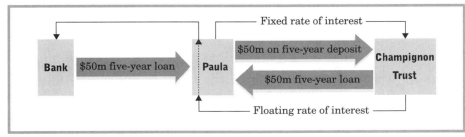

Figure 10.2

The structure of a coupon swap to hedge a bank loan

the interest rate on her bank loan. Since both rates are six-month Libor and both are fixed on the same date, Champignon Trust is effectively paying the interest on Paula's bank loan. The net effect of the arrangement is thus that Paula pays the fixed rate of interest to the trust. The rate is fixed for five years. Paula no longer has any interest rate risk because of her bank loan.

The foregoing is one example of how Paula's deal might be structured. But she might not always be fortunate enough that the rate she pays on her loan is simply a Libor rate. Let us assume that the interest rate Paula has to pay to the bank is not the same as the rate she receives from the trust. Say the rate she has to pay the bank is six-month Libor plus 2 per cent, while the rate she receives from the trust is six-month Libor. The fixed rate she pays will, of course, always be the swap rate quoted on the day.

Based on the latter scenario, Paula will pay 2 per cent more to the bank than she receives from the trust. However, that premium will remain unaltered throughout the period of the loan. The Libor element will remain the same. If Libor goes up by one basis point, she will pay one basis point more on the loan, but she will also receive one basis point more from the trust. Keep in mind however, that she is also paying the fixed rate of interest to the trust. It is therefore misleading to focus only on the one leg of the swap.

We do not know what the swap rate is that she will be paying to the trust. Therefore, we can only generalize about the effect of six-month Libor fluctuations on her hedge. Assuming for the purpose of the example that the swap rate she pays is greater than the Libor she receives:

■ if Libor rises, Paula's receipts from the trust will increase and her net payment to the trust will decrease; her instalment to the bank will increase by the same amount that her net payment to the trust decreases. Consequently, her total net cost will remain the same;

■ if Libor falls, Paula's receipts from the trust will decrease while her net payment to the trust will increase; her instalment to the bank will decrease by exactly the same amount that her net payment to the trust increases. Consequently her total net cost will remain the same.

From the summary, it is clear that Paula's position is fully and perfectly hedged. Whether interest rates rise or fall, her position remains the same. The obvious advantage to her is that the budget that forms part of her business plan is stable and safe from adverse moves in interest rates. To achieve this took a bit of planning. When she negotiated the bank loan, she knew it would be to her advantage to hedge the interest rate. Obviously, adverse moves in interest rates on such a large sum of money would have a considerable deleterious effect on her business. She therefore saw to it that the terms of the loan were such that it could readily be coincidental with the terms of a swap.

The first and most important principle in the business of hedging is therefore to keep hedging in mind at all times. When you negotiate any transaction that involves price risk of any nature to yourself, always structure the deal in such a way that it will be readily hedgeable.

Case Study 10.2

Hedging asset and liability disparities with an asset swap

We can now look at the other side of the coin. Champignon Trust must surely also have had good reasons to enter the swap. We know that Paula has fully protected herself against interest rate risk, but does that make Champignon the loser in the deal? People will tell you that derivatives markets are zero-sum markets. That means that for every winner there is an equal loser. That statement is quite true. However, the situation is not as simple as that. Let us investigate the Champignon's situation before we discuss the zero-sum problem.

Champignon's Background

Champignon is a very big trust. Its deal with Paula represents only one of various deals it does in the course of its business. Let us say, for the purposes of our example, that the Paula deal takes care of $50 million of its capital at risk. This represents only a portion of its capital, but it is the portion we will discuss.

Champignon Trust owns a large construction and development company that develops residential property. In the housing estates it sells plot and plan, turnkey deals that include whatever sort of mortgage finance the customers require. The mortgage bonds are for 20–30-year periods, with six-monthly interest rate adjustments, based on six-month Libor.

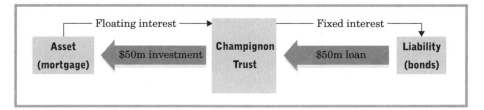

The interest rate exposure of Champignon Trust

Although the trust has great capital resources, it finds it necessary from time to time to issue five-year bonds to raise money to finance its property development activities. Champignon's interest rate exposure can thus be summed up by saying that it has asset (mortgage) based floating rate income against which it has fixed interest rate liabilities (bonds). The situation is illustrated in Figure 10.3.

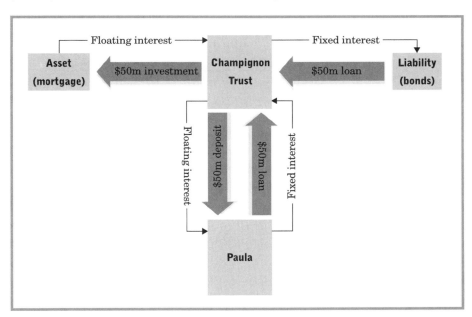

The total cash flow configuration of a hedge using an asset swap

The Interest Rate Risk

The consequent risk that the trust faces is that interest rates, specifically six-month Libor, will fall. When interest rates decline, the income diminishes, but the expenses of servicing the interest on the bonds remain the same. The trust therefore wished to protect itself against a fall in six-month Libor. For the reasons mentioned, it structured the deal with Paula in the particular way outlined above. Champignon's situation after the swap is illustrated in Figure 10.4.

The Effect of the Hedge

As already stated, in the normal course of events the trust would suffer losses if six-month Libor declined, since that would affect its income. In the previous example, we saw that in the swap with Paula, the trust faced the risk that six-month Libor would rise. That was due to the fact that it was paying the floating interest leg which was six-month Libor. This risk in the swap is thus directionally opposite to the risk of the trust in the normal course of business.

The period of the swap is not exactly the same as the period of the six-month Libor risk emanating from its income-generating mortgages because the mortgages range from 20 to 30 years. However, the risk is generated by the mismatch between the interest payments (fixed vs. floating) of the bonds and the mortgages. The bonds have a five-year maturity. The interest rate risk therefore ceases when the bonds mature. This coincides with the maturity of the swap. Of course, the trust may have to make a new bond issue to finance the repayment of some or all of the present bond issue. That in fact amounts to a rollover and it will be able to negotiate a further swap at that time to cover that bond issue.

The periodicity of the swap and that of the mortgages coincide exactly. The interest rate risk is thus fully covered in that respect. The risk is also fully covered as far as the quantitative measure is concerned, although, as previously mentioned, the trust's capital requirements are actually greater than that represented by the one swap that we are dealing with here. The risk index is identical inasmuch as both are linked to six-month Libor.

The swap therefore constitutes a perfect hedge also from the point of view of Champignon Trust.

The Zero-Sum Objection

This objection by some people is really based on fear. It is part of the fear of derivatives that we have mentioned a few times already. It is quite true that what one party loses on derivatives the other party will gain. If we speculate in the markets, whether it is in derivatives, stocks, bonds or cattle, the result is the same. What we gain, someone else must lose.

However, if we observe the situation set out in Case Study 10.1 and Case Study 10.2, we get a different perspective. The examples examine the same swap from both parties' point of view. Neither party won nor lost. That is because they were both in the market to hedge. Since their positions were carefully chosen, they both got what they came to the market to get – price certainty and price stability.

Hedging foreign borrowings with a currency swap

I have mentioned my friend Dave Lubowsky. He is the guy who owns a chain of franchised hardware outlets. As I explained earlier, he imports great quantities of hardware items from Japan and repackages them for distribution to the franchized outlets in the US.

The Background

At one stage, Dave was offered the opportunity to purchase shares in his major Japanese supplier. Apart from gaining shares in the supply company, the deal would enable some of the money he would invest to be used to upgrade the facilities of the factory. He was able to raise a loan in Japan of ¥2,970 million at a favourable fixed interest rate of 6.75 per cent per annum. The loan was for a period of two years with interest payable quarterly in arrears.

Dave's revenue was exclusively in dollars. He knew that with the increased output from the supplier and given his present profitability, he would comfortably be able to accumulate the approximate $27 million from sales over the next two years in order to repay the loan. Servicing the interest would also not present a problem. The interest would run to approximately ¥50,118,750 per quarter, which at the current exchange rate then of 109.6170 would require him to pay $457,217 every three months. Dave had done his calculations carefully and the deal was definitely worth his while (*see* Figure 10.5).

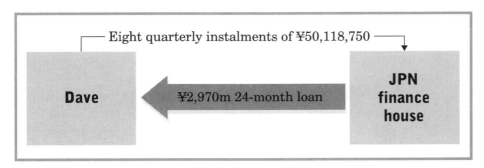

Figure
10.5

The structure of Dave's foreign loan

The risk Dave faced was that the yen would substantially appreciate against the dollar. This would invalidate all his calculations and throw his plans into disarray. If the dollar devalued against the yen, Dave would have to increase the price of his products in the US just to service interest and to eventually repay the principal on the loan. Such a price rise would make his products totally uncompetitive in the marketplace, dropping his total sales, curtailing his revenue and even jeopardizing the whole enterprise.

Consequently, the moment he arrived stateside he approached his bank to arrange a swap. The swap they managed to arrange for him is the one explained in Chapter 4. We are now in a position to look at the total structure of Dave's position in order to evaluate his hedge (*see* Figure 10.6).

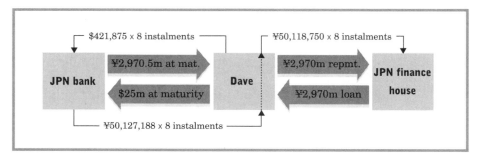

Figure 10.6

Hedging an offshore loan through a currency swap

Evaluating the Hedge

The first fact that immediately grabs our attention is that the quantitative measure of the swap risk is not equal to the quantitative risk on the loan. The rest of the elements, namely the period, periodicity and risk index, are all identical. The question that arises is whether the quantitative difference creates any problem in the hedge.

The disparity came about as a result of the time lapse between the securing of the finance in Japan and the arranging of the swap through the bank in Atlanta. Fortunately for Dave, the yen had further devalued against the dollar in the interim. It could easily have been the other way round. Being a prudent businessperson, he had considered these eventualities in his calculations. Thus, in his original studies, he had allowed for a capital repayment of $27 million.

Because Dave makes his calculations primarily in dollars, he tends to round off in dollars. When he visited his bank, he realized that, due to the move in exchange rates $25 million would be adequate. In fact, $25 million would give him ¥500,000 more than he required. Because the instalments of the swap are based on the principal, it follows that the instalments received in yen will, in their turn, be greater than those required for the loan. In the event, the total yen received through the swap would exceed the total yen instalments by ¥67,504 over the period.

The dollar instalments are obviously tailored to equate the higher yen instalments of the swap. The risk created by the swap is that the dollar would increase against the yen. This risk would be offset against the opposite risk of the loan, namely that the yen would revalue against the dollar. Because of the quantitative mismatch that now exists between the swap and the loan, Dave is exposed to naked currency risk.

The Naked Risk

Dave's naked risk amounts to an exposure to adverse moves in the exchange rate on ¥67,504. However, Dave is unconcerned. Since the interest rate on the swap is fixed, he knows that the yen income on the swap will always exceed the yen instalment he has to pay on his loan. He is therefore safe in the knowledge that the Japanese bank that is counterparty to the swap is in effect servicing the interest on the loan, with a little change left over. It is really only the value of the change that affects him. He also knows that whatever happens, he has to pay a total of $3,375,000 in interest to the swap over the next two years. Nothing will change that.

In his original calculations, Dave estimated that servicing the interest on the loan would cost him $3,657,736. Because of the favourable rate move in the interim, he will save a total of $282,736 in interest payments. Because the exchange rate of the principal in the swap was fixed at the outset, he is assured that repaying the principal can cost him no more than $25 million. He also knows that in return he will receive ¥2,970.5 million, which is ¥500,000 more than he requires to repay the loan. The slight quantitative mismatch and concomitant currency risk consequently does not bother him at all.

Hedging foreign borrowings with a cross-currency coupon swap

Case Study 10.4

Dave was fortunate, in the previous example, to have been able to arrange finance on a fixed interest rate basis. We must ask ourselves what the situation would have been had he raised the finance on a floating interest rate basis. We will assume all else remains the same.

Dave's currency risk would be the same in all respects as in the previous example. He would, however, face an additional interest rate risk. When he negotiated the loan with the Japanese finance house, he would have ensured that the interest rate was linked to some readily hedgeable rate. Since the finance house required quarterly interest payments, the obvious rate to link it to would be the yen three-month Libor. It would probably be that Libor plus a few basis points.

The swap agreement would then require a few changes. Apart from the currency risk, Dave's risk would be a rise in the yen three-month Libor. In order to cover his currency risk through the swap, he would still pay the dollar leg of the swap and receive the yen leg. The question is really whether he would be the payer or the receiver of the fixed interest rate. If he were the receiver of the fixed interest leg, he would risk a rise in the interest rate. If interest rates rose, he would pay more and that would make the swap more expensive to him. A rate rise is the same risk as he faces in the loan. Since the two risks are directionally equivalent, they would not hedge each other. Dave should therefore pay the dollar fixed interest rate leg and receive the yen floating rate leg. The complete hedge is illustrated in Figure 10.7.

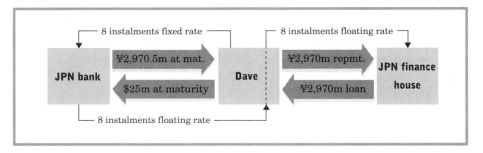

Figure 10.7

A hedge of a foreign floating interest loan using a cross-currency coupon swap

Evaluating the Hedge

A glance at Figure 10.7 will show that the hedge is as effective as ever. The income stream from the floating rate yen leg of the swap is now no longer necessarily greater than the yen required to pay the loan. This is because the floating leg, although based on a slightly larger amount of principal, is equal to three-month Libor, but the interest on the loan is three-month Libor plus some basis points.

The swap will be a par swap. This means that the fixed rate that Dave pays on the dollar leg will be the swap rate, which, as we know, is of such a magnitude as to make the swap valueless to both parties. This effectively means that the net present value of the dollar leg is equal to the net present value of the yen leg. If the yen devalues against the dollar, the net present value of that leg will diminish and the swap will become an expense to Dave. The greater the devaluation of the yen, the greater the expense to Dave. Because the yen leg of the swap and the interest on the loan are linked to the same interest rate index, Dave will be compensated for the increase by a decrease in the expense of paying the interest on the loan. He will need fewer dollars to purchase the yen required to service the interest on the loan.

The Mismatch in Principal

The original mismatch in the principal of the loan and the principal of the swap will now play a more significant role. The effect will be that when the swap becomes more expensive to Dave, his additional expense will not be matched exactly by the decrease in expense on the loan. That is because his increase in expenditure is calculated on ¥500,000 more than what his decrease in expenditure is based on. The expenses on the loan will thus decrease by fewer dollars than the expenses on the swap will increase. Against that, if the yen were to revalue against the dollar, the gain on the swap would be greater than the loss on the loan. In the result, the ¥500,000 mismatch is probably insignificant for a guy like Dave, given the amount involved. What you lose on the swings ...

Using OTC Options

Unlike swaps, options can be used to hedge a single period exposure as well as periodicity exposure. In order to demonstrate the use of options in hedging the price of money, we need to make a short digression to deal with some peculiarities of interest rate options.

Elements of Interest and Currency Rate Options

The three basic elements of these options are first, the amount of principal involved, second, the underlying rate index, and third, the strike rate. This is in line with the universal principles of all options.

The Principal
All options are given in respect of a specified quantity of the underlying. Although the underlying of an interest rate option is an interest rate index, there can be no quantitative value of an interest rate unless that rate is applied to a specific 'quantity' of money. The same considerations apply to currency options. Because the underlying is a rate, it has quantitative value only if it can be related to a principal amount. The first slight deviation encountered in options on the price of money is thus that there is a specified quantity of principal involved, which is not strictly speaking a quantity of the underlying.

The underlying

As we have said, the underlying of an interest option must be an interest rate index, such as Libor. The underlying of a currency option is an exchange rate between two specified currencies. The exchange rate is market driven and fluctuates from time to time. It therefore serves as a rate index of value for the option. For the hedger, the underlying rate index of the option must be the same as the rate index that generates the risk being hedged. For example, if the floating interest rate that you wish to hedge is six-month Libor, you need a six-month Libor option.

The implication of buying, for example, a three-month maturity, six-month Libor, European-style option is that the date at which the option can be exercised is specified and it will be three months from the initial date of the option. If it were an American option, it could be exercised at any time within that three-month period.

Interest rate and currency options are cash settled. This will be illustrated by example below. It means however, that you do not receive the underlying when the option is exercised. You are paid an amount of cash, which is equal to the amount by which the option is in the money. This leads us to the next quirk of options on the price of money – the determination of the strike price.

The Strike Price

You will recall that the strike price of an option is probably its most important element. Since the underlying of an interest rate option is an interest rate, we refer to its strike price as a strike rate. Incidentally, the same holds true for a currency option, where the strike price is similarly referred to as the strike rate because the underlying of the option is an exchange rate.

By the strike rate of an interest rate option, the option writer guarantees that rate as being the rate at which the option holder will be able to transact a loan or an investment at some specified future time. In a currency option, the option writer guarantees to the option holder that the strike rate of the option is the exchange rate at which the holder will be able to buy or to sell the one currency against the other currency mentioned, should he exercise the option.

In a borrower's option, the strike is guaranteed as the rate at which the holder will be able to borrow the principal sum of the option at a date in the future. In a lender's option, the strike rate is guaranteed as the rate at which the holder will be able to invest the principal sum of the option at a date in the future.

In a European-style option, that date in the future is the expiration date of the option. An option will therefore have a life, or a period to maturity, for as long as the parties agree. The hedger will obviously take care that the option expiration coincides with the rollover date of the loan or investment that is being hedged. Alternatively, option expiry will be at the anticipated date of the loan or investment.

The option at expiration

If, at option expiration, six-month Libor is higher than the strike rate, the holder will exercise the option. The option writer does not necessarily guarantee to give the holder a loan, or that he will be able to get a loan anywhere else. Only the specified Libor at the specified time in the future is guaranteed.

In the example, therefore, if the holder of the option were to borrow money, he would have to borrow it at the current six-month Libor. The writer of the option will pay the option holder the difference between the total interest the holder will now have to pay on a loan of the principal and what he would have had to pay had six-month Libor been equal to the strike rate. Whether or not the option holder actually borrows any money from anybody is irrelevant to the option transaction. The option is cash settled and has no further conditions attached.

On the other hand, if, at option expiration, six-month Libor is lower than the strike rate of the option, the option holder will walk away from the option. He will forfeit the premium paid.

The Strike Rate and the Option Premium

When the bank or other writer of an option on the price of money determines the strike rate, which in turn determines the option premium, it must calculate it against a benchmark rate. One obviously expects that the current market price of the underlying must serve as the benchmark, as with all other options. Surprisingly, this is not so in this case.

The FRA Rate

The benchmark against which the strike rate of an option is measured is the current FRA rate. Forward rate agreements are special instruments that were created by banks to refine certain problems encountered by ordinary forward contracting on interest rates. FRAs are by definition agreements that relate to loans or investments in the future. A client might require a loan in one month's time. The loan he requires is for a six-month period. The bank would enter into a forward rate agreement with him and quote him an interest rate based on that requirement. In market terminology, the deal would be referred to as a 1s-7s FRA. A six-month loan required in three months' time would evoke a different FRA rate quote from the bank. The latter deal would be known as a 3s-9s FRA.

The resemblance between the FRA rate and the strike rate must now be apparent. Consider the situation at the start of the period, when the option between the hedger and the bank is being negotiated. Assume we require a three-month maturity option, with six-month Libor as underlier. Like a FRA, this option requires a rate that reflects the cost and risk elements involved in guaranteeing a rate that will be effective from a date three months hence, for a six-month period thereafter. It equates exactly with the appropriate considerations for a 3s-9s FRA. The strike of the option will thus be determined with regard to the current 3s-9s FRA rate rather than the current six-month Libor rate.

It stands to reason that no Libor rate will be equal to any FRA rate because Libor is the current market rate – it is today's fixing for six-month Libor. That means that it is the rate at which banks will agree to grant a loan today, running from today for a period of six months. The 3s–9s FRA rate is also a rate for a six-month loan, but not a loan running for six months from today. It is the rate for a six-month loan running from a date three months from today. There is no way that these two rates could ever be the same.

Determining the Option Premium

As we already know, the option premium is determined by a number of factors, but the most important, especially at the start, is whether the option is ITM, ATM or OTM. Thus, we come to the second peculiarity of interest rate options. The strike is not determined with reference to the current market rate of the underlier. This means that the option will be ITM, ATM or OTM with reference to the appropriate FRA rate. How this situation influences the hedger will be demonstrated in the examples that follow.

This latter peculiarity is shared also by a currency option. The strike and premium will be calculated with reference to the present forward rate for that currency and not with reference to the current rate of exchange of that currency.

As a generalization, one can say therefore that options on the price of money will have strike rates and premiums determined by reference to the forward rates of their underliers and not their market rates. At expiration, however, the option strike rate will be compared and related to the current market rates of the underliers.

Case Study 10.5

Hedging a single-period interest rate exposure with an interest rate swap

A property investment company in the UK has sold off one of its lesser performing properties for £1,500,000. The treasurer of the company expects the transfer of the property to go through and the purchase price to be received in less than one month's time. He is also aware that the company is in the process of buying some industrial property just outside Oxford. He has been informed that the finalization of that purchase will take at least another eight or nine months.

He therefore knows that he will have to invest the proceeds of the sale temporarily, pending their use in the Oxford purchase. His investment will be linked to six-month Libid (London Inter-Bank Bid Rate). However, any derivative instrument that he can use to hedge his position will be linked to Libor and not to Libid. The present six-month Libor rate is 7.12 per cent. The 1s-7s FRA is 7–6.9 per cent.

His concern is that interest rates may drop and when he receives the money he will not be able to obtain such a favourable investment rate. On the other hand, should interest rates rise, he does not wish to lose the opportunity to invest at an even better rate. He consequently decides to investigate the feasibility of an anticipatory hedge, using an OTC option.

He further decides that it would be safe for the option to have a one-month maturity. It would be a serious blunder to have the option expiration prior to his receiving the money to invest since it would be better to make the investment concurrently with the settlement of the option. He also considers it safe to invest the money for six months. The expected need for the money would not arise before then. If, closer to the end of six months, it became clear that the money would still not be required, he could always roll the investment over for another shorter period.

The first question that he has to resolve is what interest rate level he should guarantee through the option. As we know, the closer the strike comes to the money, the higher the premium. The present six-month Libor rate is somewhat higher than the 1s-7s FRA level. This means that an option strike at the present Libor level will be slightly in the money by 0.12 per cent (7.12–7 per cent). A slightly ITM lender's option for one month would not normally be prohibitively expensive.

The property investment company treasurer telephones a few of the banks that he normally deals with, requesting an indication premium for a lender's option to guarantee the present Libor level of 7.12 per cent p.a. The best quote he gets is an indication rate of 14 basis points per annum (14bp p.a.). One 100 basis points equals 1 per cent. Quotes are mostly given in basis points per annum, but some banks may quote a flat rate. Watch for this difference when comparing quotes.

He now calculates the total premium he will have to pay for the option. The principal is £1,500,000. The interest rates and the premium quote are all annualized, so he has to recalculate them back to the one-month maturity period of the option that he requires. The actual period for which he will require the option before he receives the money will be 30 days. This is therefore the period that he uses in his calculation of the premium.

$$\frac{£1,500,000 \times 30 \times 0.14}{365 \times 100}$$

The total premium comes to £172.60. It is payable upfront. The actual cost to the company is therefore £173.61, or 14.08 basis points:

$$£172.60 + \left[\frac{172.60 \times 30 \times 7.12}{365 \times 100}\right]$$

He decides that this is an insignificant amount and decides to take the option.

Scenario 1: interest rates drop

At the end of 30 days, six-month Libor is at 6.15 per cent. The option is in the money by 0.97 per cent p.a. (7.12 per cent – 6.15 per cent). The bank that wrote the option now has to cash settle it since the treasurer exercises the option. The cash settlement value comes to £7,175.34, calculated as follows:

$$\frac{£1,500,000 \times 180 \times 0.97}{365 \times 100}$$

However, the company receives the settlement amount on the expiry date because the option is in sterling. The actual amount is therefore discounted back 180 days for early settlement and the company is paid an amount of £6,961.28.

By now, the treasurer has received the money and he invests £1,500,000 at the current Libid rate of 6.15 per cent p.a. The effectiveness of the hedge and its true cost can now be calculated. If the company had invested the £1,500,000 at 7.12 per cent (the hedged rate) for six months, the total interest received would have amounted to £52,668.49:

$$\frac{£1,500,000 \times 180 \times 7.12}{365 \times 100}$$

As it happens, the total interest received amounted to £45,493.15, to which must be added the £7,175.34 option settlement. The total received in interest and settlement therefore amounts to £52,668.49, which exactly equals the hedged amount. The total cost amounted to £173.61, which means that the net interest receipts on the hedged transaction was £52,494.88. Effectively, the hedged rate was thus 6.98 per cent p.a.

Scenario 2: interest rates rise

At the end of 30 days, six-month Libor is standing at 8.1 per cent. The treasurer does not exercise the option and instead allows it to lapse. He invests the £1,500,000 at 8.1 per cent and his gross interest receipt on the investment amounts to £59,917.81. When the option premium of £173.61 is subtracted, the net receipt comes to £59,744.20. The company thus effectively obtained an investment rate of 7.96 per cent p.a.

Note: although it was insignificant in the above example, it is important to calculate the true cost of the option by taking into account the interest on the premium for the duration of the option. On longer-term options, this calculation can make a significant difference to the cost of the hedge. In addition, for the purposes of the example, it was assumed that the Libor and the Libid rates were the same. This would never be the case. There might therefore have been some small movement in the basis between the two rates. This would have affected the hedge only marginally. The principle demonstrated is correct however.

Hedging a bank loan with an interest rate cap

Case Study 10.6

A meat packing company, situated in Aberdeen, Scotland has identified a need to enlarge its vacuum-packing facility. This involves not only the purchase of new machinery and equipment, but also additions to its existing buildings. The total project has been properly costed out and the company has approved a capital budget of £6,500,000. This capital budget includes a 5 per cent reserve for incidental costs. The board has decided that £5 million will be financed through a bank loan.

The loan was negotiated with the bank for a period of two years, with the interest rate linked to six-month Libor. The company is concerned that its careful budgeting of the project will be upset should interest rates rise beyond the 1 per cent p.a. 'cushion' it has built in. On the other hand, the company wishes to avail itself of any opportunity of saving on its cash flow budget.

The company's treasurer consequently decides to obtain indication prices for a two-year interest rate cap with six-monthly Libor rollovers. He requests a strike 1 per cent out of the money. The company's cash-flow budget is based on a six-month Libor-linked rate. It based its budget calculations on six-month Libor being at 6.45–7.45 per cent. At the time of the treasurer's enquiries, six-month Libor is fixed at 6.55 per cent. The semi-annual swap rate is 6.40–6.30 per cent. The best quote the treasurer can get is 1.75 per cent of the notional principal, payable upfront. The notional principal is also referred to as the face value of the option.

Face value	£5 million
Maturity	Two years
The underlying	Six-month Libor
Strike rate	7.40 per cent – 1 per cent away from the swap rate
Benchmark rate	The swap rate of 6.40 per cent
Premium	£87,500 – 1.75 per cent of £5 million
Start date	To coincide with the date of the loan

Table 10.1

The structure of the interest rate cap obtained by the property investment company treasurer

The company obtains an interest rate cap, structured as set out in Table 10.1.

Evaluating the Hedge

The interest rate that the company will pay on the loan is now 'capped' at 7.4 per cent interest per annum. This is 0.05 per cent better than the worst-case scenario for which it budgeted. The periodicity of the loan will equal the periodicity of the cap. Every six months on the rollover date of the company's loan and cap, the cap's strike rate of 7.4 per cent will be compared with the six-month Libor fixing on that day.

To illustrate the point, assume that on a particular rollover date six-month Libor is fixed at 8 per cent. The writing bank will calculate the settlement amount as follows:

$$\frac{£5,000,000.00 \times 180 \times (8-7.4)}{365 \times 100} = £14,794.52$$

However, the £14,794.52 will have to be discounted back for early settlement at the then current six-month Libor:

$$\frac{£14,794.52}{1 + \left[\frac{(8 \times 180)}{365 \times 100}\right]} = £14.233$$

Should six-month Libor be less than 7.4 per cent, the company will merely refix its loan at the current lower rate for the next six months.

Cost of the Cap

The cost of the cap is quite high. The premium amounted to £87,000 for two years of cover. At the capped rate of interest, capitalized semi-annually, the total cost of the cover amounts to £100,539.38. This represents slightly more than 2 per cent of the face value. However, the capital budget provided a 5 per cent reserve for incidental costs. The treasurer financed the premium from this reserve, which still leaves him with a 3 per cent margin for further incidental costs of the project.

Using Futures

When hedging the price of money through the use of futures, there are a number of special factors to keep in mind. In the following sections we will deal with the availability of contracts as well as some of the peculiarities encountered before moving on to examine some examples in detail.

There are a number of special features and factors to consider in using futures to hedge interest rates. With the exception of some futures contracts such as the three-month Libor contract on the Liffe, the other contracts all relate to government bonds. It is therefore necessary to investigate some of the elements of bonds in order to understand how they are used to hedge interest rates. This is therefore explained under a separate section.

As far as currency futures are concerned, the major market is the Chicago Mercantile Exchange (CME). They trade a wide variety of currencies against the dollar. Any two currencies can obviously be linked to each other through the dollar. Some of the peculiarities of these contracts will also be discussed under a separate heading.

Interest Rate Futures

There are a number of futures contracts that allow the hedging of interest rates. In the UK, the Liffe offers short-term interest rate contracts on three-month Libor in sterling and a number of other European currencies. Long-term interest rates are covered by contracts on government bonds issued by the UK as well as the German, Italian and Japanese governments.

In the US, the CBOT offers futures on US Treasury bonds (T-bonds), Treasury notes (T-notes) and Treasury bills (T-bills). These have been the basic interest rate hedging instruments in the US for many years. The CME offers a wide range of interest rate futures and options, with contracts based on the eurodollar, euroyen, Libor, eurocanada, one-month Libor and a number of foreign government bonds.

The US T-bond contract has the 30-year Treasury bond as underlier and is therefore a long-term interest rate instrument. Most government bonds have a similar pricing structure, although there may be differences in detail. They are all issued with a par value. This is the face value of the bond, which, in the case of a US Treasury bond, is $1,000.

The coupon rate is the interest rate paid by the government on the bond. The holder of a US Treasury bond with an 8 per cent coupon will therefore receive an interest payment of $80 per annum for the life of the bond. It is important to keep in mind that whatever may happen to interest rates during the life of that bond, $80 per annum is what will be paid – no more, no less.

There are two basic features with which you must come to terms in order to understand these interest rate instruments. The first feature is that bond-based futures do not strictly speaking have an interest rate yield. For our purposes, we can disregard those interesting calculations that treat them as if they do. Bond futures represent capital. The second feature, which is a direct result of the first, is that bond prices move inversely to interest rates.

The Inverse Relationship of Bonds to Interest Rates

Let us start by looking at the underlying bond. Consider an outstanding US Treasury bond and ignore, for the moment its period to maturity. Its coupon is 8 per cent, i.e. it pays 8 per cent interest on the nominal capital amount of the bond which is, as we have said, $1,000. That was the interest rate at the time that the government concerned issued the bond. Meanwhile, interest rates have risen. Comparable bonds are presently issued with a 9 per cent coupon.

A simple question now arises. If the holder of the outstanding bond wished to sell his bond, what price would he be able to realize in the market? Obviously, bond buyers do not really care what particular bond they buy. Their main concern is that they want a bond that will give them a 9 per cent return on the money they pay for it. If the holder of the outstanding bond had purchased it at issue, he would have paid $1,000. He would thus be assured of an 8 per cent return on his investment.

Now consider how the holder would be able to sell the bond. He would be able to find a buyer for his bond only if he charged a price such that the buyer would receive a 9 per cent return on that price. He would have to sell it for less than he paid for it. Obviously, if a buyer paid him $1,000 for it, the buyer would get only an 8 per cent return. Because interest rates have risen, the price of the bond has thus fallen. The opposite holds true when interest rates fall. Hence the inverse relationship between bond prices and interest rates.

Price Quotes on Bonds

From the above discussion it follows that since the interest payment on a bond never changes, it is the value of the bond that will fluctuate with variations in interest rates. The $1,000 face-value bond will no longer be worth $1,000 if interest rates fall. On the other hand, should interest rates rise that same bond may be worth more than $1,000. Its value will be determined between the difference by the coupon of the bond and the current interest rate.

There are many outstanding bonds in the market since they are continually issued and have lifetimes of ten years and more. To make things easy, the par value of a bond is always 100. This is shorthand for stating the obvious – its par value is 100 per cent of its value at the coupon rate. The present price of a bond is always quoted as a percentage of par. In other words, if a $1,000 bond drops in price to $990, its price will be quoted as 99. If its value rises to $1,100, it will be quoted as 110.

It would be too much to expect that prices would always be that easy to understand – how would one otherwise be able to confuse laymen? Interest rate and value changes will obviously not always result in whole numbers. The price quote must therefore provide for fractions. Bond prices are quoted in 32nds of a per cent. Therefore, do not be surprised when you see a bond price of 94-16. This translates as 94 and $^{16}\!/_{32}$ of a per cent.

Time to Maturity and Yields

Before being accused of oversimplification, let me immediately add that although the above argument is correct, it is not solely interest rates that determine the value of a bond. Its time to maturity must also be factored in. The price of the bond is therefore linked to its yield, a value that factors in both interest rates and time to maturity. Consequently, you will find that a $1,000 bond with an 8 per cent coupon and one year to maturity might drop to a price of $990 when interest rates rise to 9 per cent. If the same bond had ten years to go to maturity, its price might drop to $935 on such a rise in rates.

There are exciting and challenging mathematical formulae that calculate the amount that the price of a particular bond must change in order to offset a change in interest rates. This need not detain us here. There are many consultants out there who are drooling at the mouth to do these calculations for you. On the other hand, any good spreadsheet has the formulae built in.

Hedging Bonds

The hedger does ultimately have a concern with the mathematics, however. The hedger must concern himself with equivalence. If you hold bonds, whether government or corporate, their values are influenced by interest rates. In order to hedge them with futures, you are going to have to determine how the bonds you hold relate to the underlying of the futures contact. In order to hedge, you must establish equivalence in value at risk and in price sensitivity.

The question of equivalence comes down to how many T-bond futures contracts you would need to hedge a particular T-bond or basket of bonds. It is beyond the scope of this book to deal with this question, but there are some extremely good booklets on this subject obtainable free of charge from, *inter alia*, the CBOT. They explain in detail how these calculations are done. On the other hand, it may be time to call in the experts.

Case Study 10.7

Hedging an intended issue of corporate bonds with futures

A software solutions corporation situated in Atlanta has decided to raise $10 million in capital through a bonds issue. During May, the final decision was made. The bonds will be issued in six months' time.

The company bases its bonds issue calculation on the fact that comparable bonds are selling at 96–16. It plans to issue bonds with a $1,000 par value. It therefore plan to issue 10,000 bonds. The cost of the issue will be the discount to par at which comparable bonds are trading. The company plans an issue cost of 3–16. In monetary terms this translates to 3.5 per cent of $10 million, which equals $350,000.

The company's concern is that interest rates will rise. If they do, bond prices will fall to below the present 96–16 level. The cost of the issue will therefore rise.

The corporation's treasurer reports that T-bond futures are trading at around 98. Should the corporation sell futures to hedge, the present futures price would give it a negative basis, which should work in its favour since it will tend to narrow during delivery month. See the previous discussion on basis. Thus the board instructs the treasurer to hedge its bond issue by using futures.

One CBOT T-bond futures contract equals $100,000 face value of US Treasury bonds that mature at least 15 years from the futures contract delivery date. The face value of the bonds that the corporation intends to issue will be $10 million.

In order to hedge this future issue the corporation must take an equal and opposite risk to the one it faces. Its present risk is a rise in interest rates based on a principal amount of $10 million. Its risk exposure is for a six-month period. From our previous discussion, it is apparent that risking a rise in interest rates is the same as risking a fall in the price of bonds – $10 million worth of bonds in this case.

In order to hedge its risk it will need to assume the risk that $10 million worth of bonds will rise in price during the next six months.

Cash market		Futures market		Basis
June 1 Budget issue price	96–16	June 1 Sell 100 T-bond futures	98–22	2–6 under

Table 10.2

The cash market and futures market position of the software solutions corporation

If you sell $10 million worth of bonds at today's price without owning them, you risk a rise in price. When you buy the bonds in the future (in order to deliver what you have sold), the price may have risen and you will make a loss. That is the risk the corporation must now assume in order to cancel out its existing risk. It must therefore sell $10 million worth of futures contracts.

On June 1 the treasurer instructs the corporation's broker to sell 100 December T-bond contracts on the Chicago Board of Trade. The broker reports back on the same day with a fill at a price of 98–22. The corporation's position is now as illustrated in Table 10.2.

Scenario 1: Interest rates rise

When the corporation's bonds are issued on December 1, interest rates have risen, so the price that it realizes on the issue is 92–2. Since interest rates have risen, T-bond futures prices have declined. On December 1, the treasurer instructs the broker to lift the corporation's hedge by buying 100 T-bond futures. His broker reports back on the same day with a fill of 93-10. The result of the corporation's hedge is now as illustrated in Table 10.3.

Evaluating the Hedge

The corporation budgeted for a cost of issue of 3–16. As things turned out with the rise in interest rates, its actual costs of issue more than doubled from 3–16 to 7–30 (100 – 92-02/32). Had it not been hedged, the issue would have been a disaster. Fortunately, the total costs were offset by a profit on the futures position of 5–12. The actual cost of issue was thus limited to 2–18 (7–30/32 – 5–12/32). The actual cost of issue was lower than the budgeted cost by 30/32 (3–16/32 – 2–18).

We can put some money figures into this discussion. Every full point in a Treasury futures contract equals $1,000. Therefore, every 32nd of a point is equal to $31.25. The total profit on the futures was 5–12, which equals $5,000 (for the five full points) plus $375 for the 12/32 of a point – total thus of $5,375 per contract. The corporation's position was taken with 100 contracts, so the total profit on the futures market was $537,500.

How much money did the corporation actually raise by means of its issue? It received 92–02/32 per cent of the $10 million face value

	Cash market		Futures market		Basis
Table 10.3	June 1 Budget issue price 96–16 Dec. 1 Attained issue price 92–02		June 1 Sell 100 T-bond futures 98–22 Dec. 1 Buy 100 T-bond futures 93–10		2–6 under 1–8 under
	Increased issue cost:	4–14	Profit realized	5–12	Basis change: + 30/32

The result of the corporation's hedge when present rates have risen

of the bonds it issued, which totals $9,206,250. To this should be added the profit on the futures, which gives a grand total of $9,743,750 raised. The total cost of the issue was thus $256,250 ($10 million − $9,743,750).

The salient point to note from this example is that the hedge itself was profitable. The hedge did not perfectly neutralize the loss on the risk – it contributed a profit. The profit was exactly equal to the positive change of 30/32 in the basis (*see* Table 10.3).

The corporation had foreseen this development, which is why it decided to hedge with futures. If you remember our earlier discussion on basis and normal and inverse markets, you must also have foreseen this development. An analysis of the situation will test the validity of the statement.

Because the cash price was lower than the futures price at the outset, it was clear that this was a normal market. In a normal market the basis will narrow and tend to zero in the delivery month of the futures. December was the delivery month (but not the delivery date) of the futures contract the corporation hedged with. The short hedger, i.e. someone who hedges by shorting the futures, will profit from a narrowing of the basis in a normal market. This can be expressed differently. The short hedger will profit from the strengthening of a weak basis. It gets even better. A short hedger will always profit if he starts off with a negative basis and holds the position to the delivery month. This statement is not a gamble, it is not a guess – it is a fact that you can take to the bank.

Scenario 2: Interest Rates Decline

When the corporation's bonds are issued, interest rates have fallen substantially. Bonds equivalent to the grade of the corporation's issue are selling at 97–30. The December futures are trading at 99–6. The results of the hedge are now as illustrated in Table 10.4.

Evaluating the Hedge

In all hedges, except with options where a premium is due, the hedged position gives a zero gain or loss result. From the start we

Cash market		Futures market		Basis
June 1 Budget issue price	96–16	June 1 Sell 100 T-bond futures	98–22	2–6 under
Dec. 1 Attained issue price	97–30	Dec. 1 Buy 100 T-bond futures	99-06	1–8 under
Decreased issue				Basis change:
cost:	1–14	Loss sustained	0–16	+ 30/32

Table 10.4

The result of the corporation's hedge when interest rates have fallen

mentioned that futures are different because of moves in the basis. In the first scenario we saw how the inevitable change in basis resulted in a profit on the hedge.

In the present scenario, the initial situation is the same as in the first one. The only difference is that interest rates declined and that, consequently, bond prices rose. This has resulted in the corporation realizing more money on its issue than it had anticipated. This increase was partly offset by the loss it suffered on the futures position. The main point again is that the basis has narrowed. Whether prices go up or down is irrelevant, the basis will tend to zero in the delivery month. Therefore, the hedge itself showed the same profit, namely 30/32nds of one point, that it did in the first scenario. The profit on the hedge is the reason why the loss on the futures was not as great as the increase in the capital raised.

In retrospect, the company would now have been better off had it not hedged. Nevertheless, considering the fiasco that would have resulted if the first scenario had materialized, not hedging is just too great a risk to take.

Currency Futures

As we have said, most currency futures trade on the CME. Many countries' own exchanges also offer contracts that trade their currencies against other currencies.

The main element to keep in mind when dealing in currency futures is how the contract is structured. On the CME, all contracts are based on the foreign currency's price in US dollars. If your 'home' currency is not US dollars, you will always have to reorient your thinking in order to take the correct position if you trade on the CME. For instance, assume that your 'home' currency is the Swiss franc and you are owed US dollars. You will tend to think of yourself as being long dollars. Your concern would be that the dollar declines in value against the franc. You would therefore wish to hedge by going short the dollar against the Swiss franc.

You can hedge your position on the CME, although you cannot short the dollar against the franc. Because the futures contract is

Swiss franc priced against the dollar, you could only go long or short the franc. You would therefore have to think of yourself being short Swiss franc, not long US dollar. Considering the situation from this perspective, your concern must be that the franc gains in value against the dollar. This is just the other side of the coin of the dollar losing value against the franc. Your hedging strategy must therefore be to buy Swiss franc futures on the CME.

Hedging foreign currency on an export transaction with futures

A UK manufacturer of electronically controlled engineering equipment negotiates an export deal with a US-based importer of such equipment. The contract price is £1,480,000, payable by letter of credit against delivery of the machinery in New York.

The UK manufacturer faces no currency risk as it will be paid in sterling. However, when payment is due, the US importer will have to convert his dollars into sterling. His concern is therefore that sterling will appreciate against the dollar. Should that happen, the transaction would cost him more dollars than he had bargained for – his cash position would be short sterling.

When the deal is negotiated, sterling is trading at $1.6130. The US importer therefore budgets on paying $2,387,240 for the equipment. The agreement provides for delivery of the equipment within four months of a firm order being placed. Consequently, the importer expects delivery some time in May.

The importer's financial director telephones the company's broker at the time it places the firm order. She discovers that June sterling futures are trading at $1.6425. The contract size is £62,500. She instructs the broker to buy 24 June sterling contracts (£1,480 000/62,500 = 23.68 – rounded up to 24). Later the same day the broker telephones her back with a fill at 1.6450. The importer's market position is now shown in Table 10.5.

The basis that is established is a negative one and the market is normal. She therefore knows that the basis will probably not favour the company as it has established a long hedge.

Sterling Appreciates

Assume that at the time payment is due, sterling has appreciated against the dollar and is trading at 1.850. The US importer purchases the sterling at the market rate and lifts the hedge at the same time. The broker reports a fill of 1.870. The result of the hedge is shown in Table 10.6.

Cash market		Futures market		Basis
Jan. 11 Short sterling	1.6130	Jan. 11 Buy 24 sterling futures contracts	1.6450	0.032 under

Table 10.5

The sterling hedged position of the US-based importer

Evaluating the Hedge

The loss on the cash position was not completely offset by the profit on the futures. Ignoring quantity by basing the calculation purely on the price in dollars per pound sterling, as indicated in Table 10.6, the profit/loss discrepancy is $0.012 (0.2370 − 0.2250). This is equal to the amount by which the basis strengthened.

However, there was a slight mismatch in the quantum of the hedge. The number of futures contracts was rounded up to 24 from 23.68. The total cash market cost of the equipment had thus increased from the anticipated $2,387,240 to $2,738,000. This represents a loss of £350,000.

Against this loss however, a profit was realized on the futures position. As indicated in Table 10.6, the profit in the futures market was $0.2250 per pound. There is £62,500 pound sterling per contract and the position was taken in 24 contracts. The total futures profit was therefore $337,500 (62,500 × 24 × $0.2250). The net cost increase of the purchase after the hedge was $12,500. The cost increase is the result of a combination of two factors – basis movement and a quantitative mismatch. In this case, the basis movement worked to create a loss, while the quantitative mismatch worked to create a profit, offsetting the loss.

Although the hedge was imperfect, its effect was minimal. In fact, it protected the importer from suffering a much greater loss. Had he not hedged, his loss would have been the full $350,760. This demonstrates again that the risk of an adverse move in the basis is a much lesser risk than naked price risk. The maximum theoretical price risk the importer faced was equal to the total original basis of $0.032 per pound sterling. This results from the fact that the narrowing of the basis in a normal market works against a long hedger.

The theoretical maximum loss could have materialized only in the unlikely event that the basis reached zero before delivery date in the delivery month. As it was, that date was still approximately one month away at the time the treasurer lifted the hedge. The theoretical maximum basis risk was therefore $47,360. The treasurer considered this acceptable under the circumstances of a no-cost hedge.

Cash market			Futures market			Basis
Jan. 11 Short sterling May 9 Buy sterling	1.6130 1.8500		Jan. 11 Buy 24 sterling futures contracts May 9 Sell 24 futures	1.6450 1.8700		0.032 under 0.020 under
Loss:	0.2370		Profit:	0.2250		Basis Change: + 0.012

Table 10.6

The result of a long hedge in foreign currency where the foreign currency appreciates

Sterling Depreciates

Let us now assume that by the time payment for the equipment has to be made, sterling has depreciated against the dollar and is now trading at $1.425 per pound. The treasurer lifts the hedge and a fill at $1.445 is reported. The importer's position is now as illustrated in Table 10.7.

Evaluating the Hedge

Because of the change in basis of 0.012, the loss on the futures is greater than the profit made in the cash market. Ignoring the quantitative mismatch again, the loss exceeded the profit by $0.012 per pound sterling ($0.20000 – $0.1880). Thus, whether prices increase or decrease, a narrowing basis will be detrimental to a long hedger in a normal market. As stated earlier, the loss due to basis movement was a pre-calculated risk, regarded as acceptable by the treasurer.

The actual price paid for the sterling was $2,109,000. This represents a $278,240 improvement on the anticipated cost. Against that, there was a loss on the futures of $0.2000 per pound, amounting to $296,000. The actual cost of the sterling was therefore $2,405,000 ($2,109,000 + $296,000). The actual cost exceeded the anticipated cost by $17,760 ($296,000 – $278,240). This was an insignificant cost compared to the risks run.

The difference in the hedge discrepancy when the price increased and decreased deserves an explanation. When the price increased, the discrepancy (the amount by which the hedge was imperfect) amounted to $12,500. At the time, we said that it was the result of two factors working against each other: the narrowing of the basis causing a loss and the quantitative mismatch (rounding up of contracts) causing a profit. If the contracts had been rounded down rather than up, the mismatch factor would have had the opposite effect.

When the price decreased, the discrepancy was greater, amount-

Cash market			Futures market			Basis
Jan. 11 Short sterling	1.6130		Jan. 11 Buy 24 sterling futures contracts	1.6450		0.032 under
May 9 Buy sterling	1.4250		May 9 Sell 24 futures	1.4450		0.020 under
Profit:	0.1880		Loss:	0.2000		Basis Change: + 0.012

Table 10.7

The US importer's position on an appreciation of sterling

ing to $17,760. Both factors – the narrowing of the basis and the quantitative mismatch – were also present in this case. However, instead of working against each other, they worked to leverage each other, which was why the discrepancy was greater.

Using Options on Futures

Since these options have futures contracts, there are no special factors to keep in mind other than the ones that apply to the underlying futures contracts. We can therefore immediately plunge into a working example. Because option prices are so intricately related to the prices of their underlying, historical prices are used in all commodity option examples.

Case Study 10.9

Hedging a foreign currency purchase with a commodity option

Derby-Fulton & Son is a US manufacturer of heavy earthmoving machinery. It decides to place an order for the supply of heavy-duty gearboxes from a manufacturer in Germany. The order is placed on July 15, 1999, for delivery at the end of October. The delivery date is specified by Derby-Fulton to meet its assembly and delivery schedule. The purchase price, which is to be paid by letter of credit against delivery, is DM9,475,000.

The treasurer and the financial director have discussed hedging. They are aware that the value of the DM has been steadily declining against the dollar since October 1998. However, looking at the price graph, they notice that there are continuous rallies of the DM before periods of relative decline. The market volatility makes it impossible for them to predict what the situation might be in four-and-a-half months' time. Although the general trend may be downwards, it may turn around completely in that period. Alternatively, the DM could be part way through a strong rally at the time when they have to buy. They thus decide that the treasurer should investigate hedging with a commodity option, which will at least leave them with some opportunity for profit should there be a further decline.

In order to hedge with an option on futures, Derby-Fulton will have to buy a call option. The reason for this is that the risk it faces in the cash market is a rise of the DM against the dollar. It must now assume an opposite hedging risk. Consequently, it needs an option that will gain in value when the DM rises in relation to the dollar. The DM contract on the CME quotes the price of DM in US dollars. Therefore, if the DM gains against the dollar, the price in dollars will be greater. The contract value is in dollars. Therefore, the dollar value will be greater. Thus, given the structure of the CME contract, the company must buy a call. As previously explained, a call option will gain in value when the price of the underlying rises.

On July 15, the treasurer of Derby-Fulton speaks to its bank and determines that spot DM is trading at $0.5195. He then telephones its futures broker who informs him that the first DM contract delivery month after the end of October is December. At that moment, December DM futures are trading at $0.52810. The call that is closest to the money is the $0.5300 option. The lower one is the $0.5200 call, which is way ITM and would be much too expensive. The $0.53000 call is trading at $0.01130.

The size of the DM futures contract is DM125,000. One option has one futures contract as the underlying. The treasurer therefore instructs the futures broker to buy 76 CME DM December 530 calls (DM9,475,000/125,000 = 75.8 – rounded up to 76). The broker calls back later and reports that the order was filled at $0.01130. The market position of the company is shown in Table 10.8.

Unlike a futures hedge, there is no basis to take into consideration. Keep in mind that it is the price of the futures that is hedged at $0.5300 and not the price of the spot. If the spot rate rises, the futures price will also rise, but we know that it will not rise cent for cent. The basis between the futures price and the strike price of the option is 0.0019. This means that the futures price must rise by 0.19¢ per DM before the option is properly ATM. Even then, real protection starts only when the futures price has risen beyond the $0.53 mark by $0.0113 (the option premium) to $0.5413. This is what is known as the breakeven point. Breakeven is when the profit on the option is sufficient to cover its cost; in other words, breakeven is when the option is ITM by an amount equal to its premium. By how much the spot price must rise before the futures price reaches breakeven is uncertain. Derby-Fulton's profit/loss profile per option is illustrated in Figure 10.8.

As the figure shows, the greatest possible 'loss' is the cost of the premium, being $1,412.50 per option ($0.01130 × 125,000), which totals $107,350 ($1,412.50 per option × 76 options) in this case.

Cash market		Futures market		Premium
July 15 Short DM	0.5195	July 15 Long at the strike of the call	0.5300	0.01130

Table 10.8

A short foreign currency position hedged with a long call

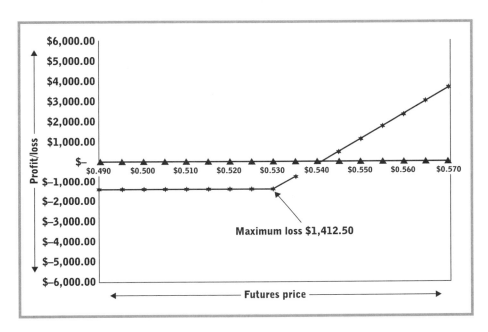

Maximum loss $1,412.50

Figure 10.8

Profit/loss profile of a $/DM call option.

Outcome of the Hedge

After July 15 the DM rises against the dollar over a period, then declines again, reaching a low of $0.5300. Thereafter it appreciates again and actually reaches a price of $0.56 before it starts falling back. During this rollercoaster ride, the treasurer experiences no stress.

On October 29 payment falls due. The bank pays the DM in terms of the letter of credit at the ruling spot price of 0.5314. On the morning of that day, the treasurer gives the futures broker instructions to lift the hedge. The broker later reports that the futures price opened at $0.54000. Therefore, the option was ITM and he exercised it. At the same time he sold 76 December DM futures. The futures orders were filled at $0.54150. This was only $0.0002 or $25 per option better than breakeven.

As a result of the exercise of the options, the company had been assigned 76 long December DM futures at a price of $0.53000. The

	Cash market			Futures market		Premium
July 15 Short DM		0.5195	July 15	Long at the strike of the call	0.5300	
Oct. 29 Buy DM		0.5308	Oct. 29	Short futures	0.5415	0.01130
Loss:		0.0113		Profit:	0.0115	

Table 10.9

Result of a long currency hedge with commodity options

short positions the broker had taken were cancelled by the long positions that had been assigned. The company's market position was now as shown in Table 10.9.

Evaluating the Hedge

When the loss in the cash market is deducted from the profit in the futures market, a result of $0.0002 is obtained. This is the same amount by which the net futures position eventually exceeded the breakeven. When the premium of the option is subtracted from that result, the net cost of the hedge comes to $0.0111 or $1.387.50 per option ($0.0111 × 125,000). The net total result of the hedge therefore does not come to a profit but seems to come to a cost of $105,450 ($1,387.50 × 76). Due to the rounding up of contracts, the calculation is not quite correct. When the number of contracts are rounded up, a profit in the futures will have a greater ameliorating effect on the loss in the cash market. It tends to cause a profit on the hedge. Under these circumstances a loss in the futures will decrease the profit in the cash market and may cause a loss on the hedge. Thus in order to come to the correct answer, we need to calculate the result in each market separately.

The company had to buy DM9,475,000. At the then ruling rate of $0.5195, the total cost would have been $4,922,262.50. The company eventually bought this amount of DM at a rate of $0.5308, paying a total of $5,029,330, thus incurring a cost increase of $107,067.50.

The profit in the futures market was $0.0115, less the premium of $0.0089, giving a net profit of $0.0026 per DM. Taking into account the 76 contracts of DM125,000 each, we get a total profit of $24,700 ($0.0026 × 76 contracts × 125,000). Offsetting this profit against the total price paid for the deutschmark gives a net cost for the DM of $5,004,630 ($5,029,330 − $24,700). This represents a net cost increase of $82,367 ($107,067.50 − $24,700).

The total premium of the options was $107,350 ($0.0113 × 125,000 × 76). In this case, the company was prepared to carry the cost of the options in return for the protection they afforded them. Its bottom line was thus really that the deutschmark should not cost it more than $0.5195 (the original ruling exchange rate) plus $0.0113 'insurance'. It was willing to pay a maximum rate of $0.5308 per deutschmark. Calculating back from the actual cost of $5,004,630 gives us a rate of $0.5282 ($5,004,630 ÷ 9,475,000). Seen in this light, the hedge was successful since it resulted in a somewhat better rate than Derby-Fulton was prepared to pay.

There are a number of factors that influence the outcome of a hedge such as this. It was a long hedge, and a basis move influences the outcome indirectly. The profit on the option, if any, depends solely on the movement of the futures price. Against that, the profit or loss in the cash market depends solely on the movement of the cash price. Since the prices of cash and futures are linked, basis movement must have an influence on the outcome, although other factors also influence events.

Exchange rates fluctuate in both markets during the course of a day. The outcome of the hedge will thus also be influenced by the time of day the DM was bought or sold in the cash market versus the time the futures were sold. Of course, the time the options were exercised is irrelevant, provided they were ITM at the time. Assignation takes place at the strike of the option no matter what.

In the next example, we will look at whether a slightly more advanced hedging strategy would have given a materially different result.

A long currency hedge with a synthetic call

The facts are identical to the previous example. In this case, the company takes a slightly different view of risk. Its first and major concern lies with protecting itself against an increase in the price of the deutschmark. It would therefore prefer to have a lower breakeven on an upward move. It would also prefer more flexibility in managing the risk. It realizes and accepts that this strategy will require more of the treasurer's time.

On July 15, when the treasurer speaks to Derby-Fulton's broker, he instructs the broker to buy 76 CME deutschmark December futures. At the same time, he instructs the broker to buy the 76 CME deutschmark 520 puts. The combined result of this position is known as a synthetic long call. If you refer to Figure 10.9, you will notice that the profit/loss profile described by the solid line is identical to the profit/loss profile described by the long call in Figure 10.8. Notice that the strike of the synthetic long call is at $0.52, which is exactly that of the long put option.

The broker later reports back that the long futures order was filled at a price of $0.528 and that he managed to buy the puts at a pre-

Table
10.10

Cash market		Futures market		Premium
July 15 Short DM	$0.5195	July 15 Long put at strike 520 July 15 Long futures at	$0.5280	$0.00890

A short currency position hedged with a synthetic long call

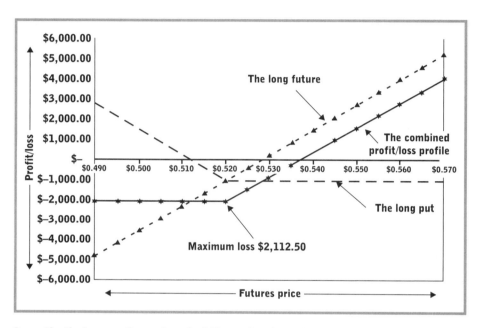

Figure
10.9

A synthetic long call constructed through a long futures position plus a long put

mium of $0.0089. Each option therefore cost a total of $1,112.50 and the total investment amounted to $84,550. The company's position is now as illustrated in Table 10.10.

Evaluation of the Hedge

The company's out-of-pocket expenses are now substantially less than the $107,350 in the previous example. Against that, however, the maximum loss that the company can suffer on a downward move amounts to $2,112.50 per option, compared with the previous example's $1,412.50. But the $2,112.50 per option does not represent an actual loss. Whatever happens, the company's out of pocket expenses cannot exceed $84,550.

The 'loss' of $160,550 ($2,112.50 × 76) is the amount that the futures price will have to drop before the company gains anything by a decline in the price of the deutschmark. This is accounted for by the fact that the long futures position was entered into at $0.008 higher than the strike of the put. When the foregoing amount is added to the option premium of $0.0089, a total difference of $0.0169 is obtained, amounting to $2,112.50 per option ($0.0169 × 125,000). When the net result of the hedge is calculated below, the effect of these figures will become more apparent.

The above situation does not bother the treasurer. A synthetic option gives him sufficient flexibility to manoeuvre out of the 'loss' situation. Should the price of the deutschmark decline seriously, the treasurer will offset the futures positions, leaving the company with only the 76 puts. Whatever loss may have been made on the futures position by then will quickly be neutralized by the puts' gain in value. This will give the company a profit in the futures market, while at the same time enjoying the advantage of purchasing the deutschmark at a lower price in the cash market.

However, let us use the historical outcome data as in the previous example. When the company's treasurer lifts the hedge on October 29, the 520 puts are not in-the-money. The treasurer therefore instructs the broker to sell the puts at the market. At the same time, the broker is instructed to short 76 deutschmark December futures at the market. The 76 futures are shorted at $0.5415, as in the previous example. The puts are sold back to the market at $0.00150. Derby-Fulton's position is now as shown in Table 10.11.

As we saw in the previous example, we must calculate the result in each market separately because of the quantitative differences. The result in the cash market will remain exactly the same as in the previous example. It is therefore necessary only to calculate the result in the futures market.

From the profit of $0.0135, the premium of $0.00890 must be subtracted. Now another advantage of this strategy presents itself. In the previous example, the long call options were exercised in order for the hedge to be lifted. Now however, the OTM puts were sold back to the market for $0.00150. The cost of the options were thereby reduced to $0.00740 ($0.00890 − $0.00150). The net profit in the futures market is thus $0.0061 ($0.0135 − $0.00740). The 76 contracts of 125,000 deutschmark each have therefore resulted in a profit of $57,950 ($0.0061 × 125,000 × 76 contracts).

This profit must be offset against the $5,029,330 that the company eventually paid for the deutschmark. The net cost of the deutschmark was thus $4,971,380, which represents an exchange rate of $0.5246.

This hedge was thus substantially better than the previous one. In this example, the cost increase was limited to $49,117.50 ($4,971,380 − $4,922,262.50), which compares favourably with the cost increase

	Cash market			Futures market		Premium
July 15	Short DM	0.5195	July 15	Long futures at	0.5280	
Oct. 29	Buy DM	0.5308	Oct. 29	Short futures	0.5415	0.00890
	Loss:	0.0113		Profit:	0.0135	Recouped: 0.00150

Outcome of a short currency hedge using a synthetic long call

of $82,367 obtained in the first example. Since none of the other facts changed, the whole 40.37 per cent improvement is purely a result of the better hedging strategy that was followed.

CHAPTER ELEVEN

Hedging Commodity and Systemic Risks

Background

Up to now we have discussed and demonstrated all the elements of hedging as well as the basic techniques. The techniques of hedging remain constant, no matter what value or variable is being hedged. The in-depth illustrations of hedging situations discussed in the previous chapter amply demonstrate all the basic techniques that apply to hedging any hedgeable risk.

Thus, in this chapter we will discuss some of the typical choices that the prospective hedger faces and strategies that can be employed when dealing with commodities and systemic risk. There would be no point in merely repeating the previous examples of hedging with different underliers, using different figures. Our purpose now is to concentrate more on those factors that influence the strategic thinking of a hedger.

Hedging Commodities

The commodity markets can be divided into three broad categories. The first and oldest is agricultural products, the second consists of metals, the third is energy. The latter category is the most recent innovation and also the fastest-growing one.

In every category of commodity you will also find a further division into primary, secondary and compound products. While the categorization of commodities will help you to identify all the sources of commodity risk in your business, the latter three divisions will be of most importance in deciding how the risk can be hedged.

Primary Commodities

A primary commodity is basically any commodity that is used as raw material. It is a commodity in its primary condition. Primary products in the agricultural sector are, for example, corn, wheat, soybeans, potatoes, livestock and so on.

A commodity must not be in its barest form or in a totally

unworked condition to be considered primary. On the contrary, they are considered primary commodities in the form that they are taken to market. Similarly, in metals it is not the ore that is the primary product but the metal itself in ingot, bar or cylinder form. Energy commodities are likewise considered primary in the condition that they are taken to market. This includes a wide variety of crude oils, pipeline natural gas, coal and units of electricity.

Not all primary products can be hedged directly. Hedging a commodity directly requires that there must be derivative instruments available that have that particular commodity as underlier. Whether any, some or all of the derivative instruments are available with a particular commodity as underlier depends on the demand therefore in the market. However, for most primary commodities all derivative instruments are available and these products can thus usually be hedged directly.

There may, however, be a difference in liquidity between different instruments on a particular underlier. You should therefore determine the liquidity of each available derivative instrument as part of the decision-making process when choosing an appropriate hedging instrument. To help you in your decision-making process, a hedging action list is given in Table 11.1. Primary commodities are nevertheless the most readily hedgeable goods.

The fact that there aren't any derivatives available for a particular commodity, is not necessarily the end of the matter. Many commodities have price moves that closely track the price moves aimed at the commodity. To illustrate the point, the prices of gold and platinum tend to track each other reasonably closely. Each of these two metals are however hedgeable in their own right. The price of copper is widely regarded as an indicator of the health of the world economy.

Secondary Commodities

Secondary commodities are those that are produced from primary commodities without substantially compounding the primary commodity with other commodities. It implies a primary product that has been through a basic process. Examples of secondary commodities in the agricultural sector are corn meal from corn, soybean meal and soybean oil as well as secondary livestock products such as pork bellies and boneless beef. In the metals market, examples of secondary products would be the many different alloys such as brass and various types and qualities of steel. In the energy market, secondary products would be refined oils such as unleaded gasoline, fuel oil, bunker fuel and the like.

There are many derivative instruments available that have secondary products as underlier. The full range of derivatives may not necessarily be available on any particular secondary product. Most of the secondary agricultural products mentioned above and many others have futures contracts offered on them. You will certainly also find cash forward contracts on those products. It is very doubtful, however, whether you will be able to find any swaps or OTC options that apply to such products. Table 11.1 should be of some assistance in guiding your actions before you hedge.

In the metals markets, you will find exchange-traded options on most of the secondary products. There are futures contracts available on unworked metals, but not on any alloys. Swaps and OTC options may be available in some isolated cases. In the energy markets futures contracts are offered on secondary products such as unleaded fuel, unleaded gasoline and fuel oil. The oil swap and OTC options markets are very active and liquid.

Again, the mere fact that there is no direct derivative instrument available on the particular product that you need to hedge is not the end of the matter. It is merely the beginning of the analysis. Secondary products can often be hedged through a hedge on the primary product, the price of which might be the major factor in determining the price of the secondary product. Table 11.1 guides you through the selection process. Additionally, if the primary product itself cannot be hedged, its price may track the price of some other commodity quite closely.

A word of caution is required, however. Whenever you hedge indirectly, there will be basis risk. In other words, there will be a difference between the price of the commodity you are hedging and the price of the commodity that is the underlying of the derivative instrument. That basis may narrow or widen from time to time. The basis will probably not be as predictable as the basis normally is in the delivery month of futures contracts. You will need to monitor the movement of the basis very closely, as its movement will determine the effectiveness of the hedge.

Compound Products

One cannot hedge the price of motor cars or of engineered parts. On the other hand, it is possible to hedge most of the primary products that go into the manufacture of these items. The price of various types and qualities of steel can be hedged through exchange traded options that are available on the London Metals Exchange. In any event, the price of pig iron, which is used in the production of steel, can be hedged, as can the price of aluminium, copper and platinum.

Every businessperson must discover and assess which prime products' prices have an influence on the well-being of the business. You must ask yourself what the primary products are that make up the price of the materials that you use all produce. The answer to this

The product	Response	Action	Result	Further action
It is a primary product	Check for availability and then for the liquidity of each available derivative instrument on the product	Contact your bank	There are liquid derivative instruments available on the product	Select the best instrument. Use the action list in Table 11.7
		Contact other banks, especially investment banks		
		Contact major suppliers such as the large oil companies	There are not liquid derivative instruments available	Use the action list in Table 11.2
		Contact a commodities broker		
		Contact a futures broker		
It is a secondary product	Check for availability and then for the liquidity of each available derivative instrument on the product itself	Contact your bank	There are liquid derivative instruments available on the product	Select the best instrument. Use the action list in Table 11.7
		Contact other banks, especially investment banks	There are no liquid derivative instruments available on the product	Try the second response in this table under secondary product
		Contact major suppliers such as the large oil companies		
	Check for availability and then for the liquidity of each available derivative instrument on the primary product	Contact a commodities broker	There are liquid derivative instruments available on the product	Select the best instrument. Use the action list in Table 11.7
		Contact a futures broker	There are no liquid derivative instruments available on the product	Use the action list in Table 11.2

Table 11.1

Pre-hedging action list for primary and secondary products

question is not necessarily simple – it may involve a number of primary products. The question is then which primary commodity, if any, has the dominant and most significant influence on the price of our inputs.

Obvious examples are electric and telephone cable. Both of these are compound products in the manufacture of which a number of raw materials are used. Nevertheless, the dominant price factor is the price of copper. Copper can therefore be used as a hedge for electric and telephone cable.

A problem of a different kind may arise. One may be a producer or user of a compound product such as fibre optic cable. There are no hedgeable primary commodities that go into the manufacture of this product. That does not mean to say that its price cannot be indirectly hedged. The demand for fibre optic cable may be linked to the demand of some other economic variable. It may be that the demand for fibre optic cable is high when interest rates are low and vice versa. It could even be linked to some economic indicator such as interest rates or the NASDAQ equity index. These are matters for investigation and research. It is a challenge that every businessperson will have to accept in order to effectively risk manage the bottom line. Table 11.2 provides some guidelines for reaching a hedging decision on products that cannot be hedged directly.

The caution concerning basis and its moves that was sounded under the previous heading is obviously applicable in this case as well. Basis risk will exist, no matter what derivative instrument is used to hedge the initial risk. In this case it is not a basis that is purely applicable to futures hedges.

From the above discussion it already becomes apparent that one need not necessarily hedge the price of a commodity or of any physical asset with a derivative instrument that has a commodity or even any physical goods as its underlier.

Hedging a Physical Asset with an Intangible

Consider, for example, the situation of a property investment company. It may have millions invested in fixed property, but the price of fixed property cannot be hedged. Nevertheless, it is a widely accepted and demonstrable fact that the prices of fixed property react to interest rates. When interest rates have a rally, the value of fixed property tends to decline and vice versa. Hedging against a rise in interest rates can therefore protect the value of fixed property.

It must also be accepted, however, that there will be certain commodities that cannot be hedged directly or indirectly. This is unavoidable in the final analysis, but the commodity derivatives markets are growing daily. A businessperson must keep an open mind, open eyes and open ears, monitoring the markets constantly

Question	Response	Action	Result	Follow-up
Is your commodity directly derived from some other commodity?	Yes	Refer to the action list in Table 11.1	The relevant commodity can be hedged	Take the action recommended in Table 11.1
			The commodity cannot be hedged	Go to the next question
	No	Go to the next question		
Is there a price-dominant primary or secondary commodity involved in your compound commodity?	Yes	Refer to the action list in Table 11.1	The relevant commodity can be hedged	Take the action recommended in Table 11.1
			The commodity cannot be hedged	Go to the next question
	No	Go to the next question		
Is there another commodity that tracks the price of your commodity or product?	Yes	Refer to the action list in Table 11.1 for that other commodity	The relevant commodity can be hedged	Take the action recommended in Table 11.1
			The commodity cannot be hedged	Go to the next question
	No	Go to the next question		
Does the demand for your commodity correlate with any economic trend that is reflected in interest rates or any equity index?	Yes	Check its hedgeability through the action suggested in Table 11.1	The trend or index can be hedged	Take the action recommended in Table 11.1
			The trend or index can be hedged	The commodity is not prsently hedgeable
	No	The commodity is not presently hedgeable		

Table 11.2

**Pre-hedging action list for commodities that cannot be directly hedged.
NB: basis risk will result**

in order to identify risk management and hedging opportunities as they arise.

Taking the Correct Hedging Position

A hedge can achieve only one of two things: it can protect against a rise in price or it can protect against a fall in price. The producer or manufacturer of any commodity always faces the risk that what he produces will decline in value. If market forces dictate that the price of the product should be lower, this will impact directly on the producer's bottom line. The producer will therefore want to protect the business against a decline in the price of the commodity or product produced.

A producer is inevitably in the rather invidious position of being a user of commodities as well. He therefore faces the dual risks of a rise in the price of raw materials and consumables and a fall in the price of the manufactured product. A manufacturer and producer of any commodity or product must always be acutely aware of both these risks and know how they should be hedged respectively.

There is another situation in which a person or a firm will want protection against a price decline. That is when existing value has to be protected against a fall in price. We have already considered the situation of a property investing company which finds itself in that position.

In all the above cases, where the manufacturer, producer or investor in physical goods faces the risk of a decline in the price of the product or in the value of the investment, the correct hedging position is to assume a risk that the price will rise. It must be well appreciated by now that these two opposite positions will cancel one another out and the original risk position will thus be hedged.

As we pointed out in the case of a manufacturer or producer of goods, the investor may often also be in a contradictory situation. The property investing company may wish to protect itself against a rise in the price of fixed property. This will be the situation when it intends to make a purchase of fixed property in the near future. Consequently the hedges that the investment company takes from time to time would have to suit each occasion. That is why so much thought and preparation should go into the making of a decision on hedging.

The consumer, user or buyer of commodities is generally in the position of being at risk of a rise in price. The commodity purchaser's hedging position will thus always be to assume the risk of a fall in price

Selecting the Correct Hedging Instrument

Every situation also calls for the correct hedging instrument to be used. Certain instruments may be more advantageous in particular circumstances than others. From the discussion thus far and all the examples that have been examined, it is apparent that a swap is probably the most totally effective hedging instrument yet devised. This is because it can be tailor-made to fit virtually every nuance of the risk that needs to be hedged.

But there are the disadvantages to a swap. It may require credit-lines to be established on both sides. Although all derivative instruments are off-balance sheet, the use of swaps may utilize a part of a firm's credit facilities. Even if this is not a problem for a particular firm, it may be that swaps are not available for hedging a particular commodity. And a swap is such a perfect hedge that it leaves no room for gain. It not only hedges away the risk of loss, it hedges away the opportunity for profit.

Most of the time this will be adequate, for instance in circumstances when a business requires predictability more than windfall profits. It is also adequate when a business wants to keep certain cash flows on budget. However, it may be totally inappropriate for certain other conditions. Swaps will, for instance, be highly inappropriate where a commodity has to be purchased for resale over a period of time. The owner of a gas station faces this situation. Should he hedge the price of fuel by means of a commodity swap for a period of two years, his station will become totally uncompetitive when the fuel price drops below the hedged level. This may in effect be ruinous to his business.

The owner of a gas station would be much better served by seeking an oil cap. Although this will in effect raise the cost of his fuel purchases by the amount of the premium, he will be in a much better position than with a swap. Depending upon the quotes he obtains, he may be able to absorb this cost. At least the oil cap will allow him to benefit when the fuel price drops below the strike of the cap by an amount that is greater than the premium.

Considering Market Conditions

When considering an appropriate hedging tool, the condition of the market should also be taken into account. Let us consider the situation of the owner of the gas station or any user of oil or oil products. All users of any commodity who wish to protect themselves against a rise in price will be long hedgers in the futures market. Normally, as we discussed, an oil cap will be a good hedging tool for a user of oil. However, one must not lose sight of the possibility of using futures. Brent crude is regarded as a benchmark price for most oils and oil products. For the purpose of illustrating the next point, we will consider the position of an oil user. The Cardiff-based company is called Rex Petrochemical Industries (RPI).

RPI manufactures chemical products from crude oil. We will assume that Brent crude establishes the benchmark of this user. The principle of what is to be explained next will remain true, no matter what commodity is actually used.

On December 10, 1999 the spot price for Brent crude was quoted at $25.42 per barrel. On the same date the open, high, low and settling prices for Brent crude futures on the IPE were as set out in

Delivery month	Open	High	Low	Settle
January 2000	$24.90	$24.91	$23.73	$24.46
February 2000	$24.01	$24.09	$23.12	$23.68
March 2000	$23.14	$23.20	$22.38	$23.20
April 2000	$22.34	$22.41	$21.70	$22.54
May 2000	$21.58	$21.67	$21.40	$21.94
June 2000	$20.95	$21.05	$20.70	$21.41
July 2000	$20.48	$20.55	$20.28	$20.99
August 2000	$20.12	$20.12	$20.12	$20.60

Table 11.3

IPE daily Brent crude futures report for December 10, 1999

Table 11.3. Note that the spot price is the highest price. January 2000, the nearest delivery month, has a lower price and the deferred months follow with prices in descending order. This is an excellent example of a market that is in backwardation – another term for an inverse market. The oil market is in fact well known as a market that is often in backwardation.

Does an opportunity lurk in this situation for RPI? They are at risk of a rise in the price of oil and, as we mentioned earlier, will be long hedgers in the futures market. You will recall that when we discussed the topic of basis, we mentioned the fact that the short hedger will make a profit on the hedge in a normal market. This hedge profit is due to a narrowing of the basis, which will tend to zero in the futures delivery month.

For the very same reason, the long hedger will make a profit on the basis move in an inverse market. Let us test this statement. Assume that RPI wants to hedge the price of its February purchases. Its order to buy IPE Brent crude futures contracts is filled at the settlement price of December 10, 1999. That is to say, it enters a long futures position in the February contract at a price of $23.68. The size of each Brent crude futures contract is 1,000 barrels. Table 11.4 sets out the hedged position of RPI.

The Oil Price Rises

On February 1 2000, RPI purchases their requirements on the spot market and they simultaneously lift the hedge in the futures. At this time the spot market price for Brent crude has risen to $27.50 per barrel. The futures price has consequently also risen and RPI's sell order is filled at $26.95. The result of the hedge is shown in Table 11.5, which demonstrates the effect that the inevitable narrowing of the basis has on the long hedge.

Table
11.4

Cash market		Futures market		Basis
Dec. 10 Short spot	$25.42	Dec. 10 Long Feb. futures	$23.68	$1.74 over

The hedged position of RPI

Table
11.5

Cash market		Futures market		Basis
Dec. 10 Short spot	$25.42	Dec. 10 Long Feb. futures	$23.68	$1.74 over
Feb. 1 Long spot	$27.50	Feb. 1 Short Feb. futures	$26.95	$0.55 over
'Loss' on spot:	$2.08	Profit on Futures:	$3.27	Change : −$1.19

The outcome of a long hedge in an inverse market, where the underlying price rises

The February 1 figures are of course my invention. For the purposes of the principles involved, this is of no consequence. The basis will have narrowed. The only question is, by how much? The oil market may even have reverted to a normal market. In that event the basis change would have been even more dramatic. The basis would then have changed from being $1.74 over to some dollars under. The result in principle would have been the same – namely a profit on the hedge – only the actual figures would have been different.

Table 11.5 illustrates that the profit on the futures is greater than the loss on spot. The profit exceeds the loss by $1.19, which is equal to the change in the basis. The so-called loss on spot is, of course, not a real loss. It is merely that the company paid more for oil in February than it did in December. The actual price that the company paid for its February oil purchase is thus $24.23 ($27.50 spot price minus $3.27 profit on futures).

A hedge is normally expected to secure the price at the level of the hedge. In this case the 'best' price that any other derivative could have hedged for RPI was the December spot of $25.42. The long futures hedge, however, predictably resulted in a lower actual price in February than the December spot. The fact that the February actual price would be lower than the December spot was predictable. That the actual saving on December spot would be $1.19 was obviously not predictable.

The Oil Price Declines

In order to demonstrate the validity or otherwise of the statement

Cash market			Futures market			Basis
Dec. 10	Short spot	$25.42	Dec. 10	Long Feb. futures	$23.68	$1.74 over
Feb. 1	Long spot	$23.78	Feb. 1	Short Feb. futures	$23.23	$0.55 over
	'Profit' on spot:	$1.64		Loss on Futures:	$0.45	Change : −$1.19

Table 11.6

The outcome of a long hedge in an inverse market, where the underlying price declines

that a hedge profit is inevitable under these circumstances, we must look at the situation where the oil price declines. Keep in mind that the basis will narrow in any event. For the purposes of our example, let us assume that the outcome of the hedge is now as illustrated in Table 11.6.

The result of the hedge is exactly the same as when the price rose. The basis narrowed by $1.19, which is also the net 'profit' on RPI's February spot market oil purchase ($1.64 − $0.45). The actual price paid by RPI for oil in February would therefore be $24.23 per barrel ($23.78 spot price plus $0.45 loss on futures) and is thus the same in this case as in the first scenario. The reason for this is that the basis change was exactly the same.

Critique of the Example

The only criticism that I have of the above figures is that if the spot price declined, it would indicate lower buying pressure. The more likely outcome of lower buying pressure would be that the market would revert to normal. That means that the futures price on February 1 would be greater than the spot price by 20 cents or so. Any situation where the futures price exceeded the spot price would necessarily imply a greater negative basis change than the one illustrated. If the basis change were more negative than the illustrated one, the hedge would have been even more profitable for RPI.

Selection Guide

Table 11.7 sets out the basic guides to selecting the most appropriate derivative instrument. Choosing the correct instrument will be an iterative process in which Table 11.7 is merely the first iteration. It is based on the assumption that all derivative instruments will be equally available for the commodity to be hedged.

The Commodity Hedge Action Lists

The action lists in Tables 11.1, 11.2 and 11.7 and are by no means

The requirement	The best choice		
The risk to be hedged consists of regular purchases or sales of a commodity over a period of time	A commodity swap	A commodity cap or floor	
The company requires a perfect hedge and waives any benefit from favourable price moves. Couterparty credit risk is acceptable	A commodity swap		
A perfect hedge is required. Waiving the benefit from favourable price moves will hurt the firm. Counterparty credit risk is acceptable	OTC options	Exchange-traded options	
A perfect hedge is required with retention of benefit of favourable price moves, but without counterparty credit risk	Exchange-traded options		
The risk is a rise in price. Market conditions are normal. Counterparty credit risk is unacceptable	Long commodity futures	Long call options on futures	Long exchange-traded options
A rise in price is faced, market conditions are normal, and a benfit from favourable price moves must be retained without counterparty credit risk	Long exchange-traded call options	Long call options on futures	Synthetic long call options on futures
The risk is a rise in price. Market conditions are inverse. A profit on the hedge is sought	Long commodity futures		
The risk is a fall in price. Market conditions are normal. Counterparty credit risk is unacceptable	Short commodity futures	Long put options on futures	Long exchange-traded options
A fall in price is faced, market conditions are normal, and a benedit from favourable price moves must be retained without counterparty credit risk	Long exchange-traded put options	Long put options on futures	Synthetic long put options on futures
The risk is a fall in price. Market conditions are normal. A profit on the hedge is sought	Short commodity futures		

Table 11.7

A first iteration action list for selecting a hedging instrument based on equal availability

exhaustive. It would be impossible, given a book of this nature, to deal with all possible permutations of commodity risks and their hedging possibilities that arise in real-life situations. Neither do they cover all possible concerns that a company might have when facing the management of a particular commodity risk.

These action lists are intended merely to serve as guidelines. We trust that they will point the business manager in the right direction and serve as useful indicators for the most appropriate procedures to be followed in coming to the correct hedging decisions.

Hedging Systemic Risk

In earlier chapters we dealt with the nature of systemic risk and how it might affect the business. The hedging of systemic risk is made possible through the use of all the available equity indices. We also discuss the fact that systemic risk from industry to industry varies.

The plurality of the indices available therefore makes it possible to correlate the systemic risk that a particular business faces with the systemic risk that is incorporated in one of the indices. In the United States, the Dow Jones Industrial Average (DJIA) is traded on the CBOT. On the CME, futures contracts on indices such as the S&P 500, the S&P Midcap 400, the S&P BARRA Value Index, and the Nikkei 225 Index are offered. Each of the indices consists of a different basket of shares. The share values of the companies are also weighted in different ways. Each of these contracts add a significant and exciting new dimension to hedging possibilities.

Hedging an Equity Portfolio

Asset management companies which manage equity portfolios normally use these indices to risk manage their portfolios. If the asset manager has a portfolio of shares with a risk profile very much like the S&P 500 index, the value of his portfolio will react to market forces in pretty much the same way as the S&P 500 does. In order to protect his equity portfolio from market forces that will cause a general decline in the shares of companies like those found in the basket that make up the S&P 500 index, the asset manager will calculate an equivalence ratio between the S&P 500 index and his own portfolio of equities. He will use this calculated to ratio to determine how many S&P 500 futures contracts will be required to hedge his portfolio. Because he must protect his portfolio from a decline in value, he will sell the number of S&P 500 futures contracts indicated by his equivalency ratio.

An asset manager may also opt for an equity swap. In this case he will enjoy the advantage of hedging the value of his own equity portfolio at its present value. He will be compensated should the average of the S&P 500 index fall below the benchmark rate established by the swap during the period from any one rollover date to the next, for the currency of the swap. However, he will have to pay whenever the average price of the S&P 500 index rises above the benchmark rate of the swap for any period. In order to achieve this situation, he will be the payer of the floating leg of the swap, while he receives the fixed rate.

Although he has thus secured his portfolio against the risk of a drop in value, he has also hedged away most of his profit opportunity. His equity portfolio might of course outperform the S&P 500 index, in which case he will still have a net gain after having made his payment on the swap. However, this type of arrangement might not be satisfactory for an asset manager who is expected to show growth over a period of time. An asset manager might therefore prefer to make use of a long put option on futures or, even better, a synthetic long put option. The latter position will give him the facility of actively managing the hedge, even allowing him to leverage the profit should there be a rise in the S&P 500 index.

Sometimes the asset manager might wish for some protection against a rise in the index. On such occasions, his concern will be that he expects to receive some funds in the near future that he wishes to be faced in his equity portfolio. Should the value of the portfolio rise in the interim, he will be able to buy fewer shares with the expected funds. His course of action then will be to buy futures contracts, thereby making a profit on a rise of the index, which he can use to augment the expected funds. The augmented funds will then have the same equity purchasing power as the original or unaugmented funds would have had, but for the rise in price.

An alternative course of action would be for the asset manager to buy call options on the index or to construct synthetic long calls. The latter courses of action depend upon the state of his funds and whether he is able to absorb the cost of the premiums on the options.

Hedging Business Risk

Every business faces the systemic risk that is inherent in the industry in which the business operates. We have discussed this previously. Just as systemic risk can be hedged out of equity risk, so that only company particular risk remains, so systemic risk can be hedged out for an individual business.

The biggest problem here is to determine what equity index most closely tracks the profit record of your business. Keep in mind that equity prices are linked in to earnings. The first iteration should therefore be to match the rise in the earnings of your business with a rise or fall in any particular index. The longer the period over which you try to make the match, the better. The iteration could also be attempted with turnover and with profits before and after tax. This is a matter that should be calculated by a specialist. The necessary correlation should be found with an existing index and an equivalency ratio calculated. This is in essence the same procedure that is followed by an asset manager.

It may well be that your business tracks the economic highs and lows of an index in a foreign country. Consider, for example, a US manufacturer that relies for the greater part of its business on orders from Japan. The size and frequency of these orders are probably influenced more by one of the Nikkei indices than by any of the domestic ones. The hotelier in Los Angeles that relies heavily on tourist traffic from Japan will probably be in the same situation. These businesses have a direct exposure to the economic ups and downs of Japan. There are thousands of businesses that face similar foreign economic exposure. But it is possible to hedge against this risk.

The first step is to determine what economic factor most closely tracks the fortunes of your business. It could be an equity index, it could be long-term or short-term interest rates, or it could be the exchange rate of your domestic currency against the foreign currency. Which ever index it is that you determine has the greatest effect on the fortunes of your business, that is the index you should use to hedge.

Consider for a moment the Los Angeles hotelier. When there's an economic down-swing in Japan, she loses turnover and profit. She takes the bed-night occupancy rate for the hotel over the past five years. She compares this to the Nikkei 225, to Japanese interest rate indices as well as to the yen–dollar exchange rate over the same period. She discovers that the Nikkei 225 correlates with the bed occupancy rate at about 0.7. Her consultants calculate an equivalency ratio between the Nikkei futures contract on the CME and her bed occupancy rate. Armed with these figures, she approaches her futures broker and proceeds to hedge a downturn in her bed occupancy rates for the period of November, December and January.

Obviously the position that she will take in the futures contracts will depend on the risk she wishes to hedge. Her concern is that the Nikkei will decline, indicating a slight downturn in the Japanese economy. She therefore risks a fall in the index, which will translate into a fall of bed-nights sold in her hotel over this period. The basic strategy might be to sell the futures contracts, thereby making a profit if the Nikkei falls, to offset against the loss of income that she will suffer as a result of the downturn. In this case, however, although she is a hedger, she does not own the underlying assets. If she takes up a futures position and the Nikkei improves, she will actually lose money on the futures without gaining any real value on an underlying asset.

In this type of situation, the hedger should always make use of options. The cost of the options must be reflected in operating costs.

Again, her best possible strategy will be to take a position of a synthetic long put. With a straight long put, she will gain if the Nikkei falls and she will be at risk only for the premium she paid, if the Nikkei rises. At the same time her hotel should be fully booked. However, with a synthetic put she will gain a greater advantage.

A synthetic put is constructed by means of a short futures position plus an at the money call option. If, after she has taken this position, the Nikkei and the Japanese economic news take a definite downturn, she can always sell back the ATM call. That will at least recoup some of the cost of the initial premium. The profit on the short futures position will therefore be greater. However, should the Nikkei and the economic news from Japan become very bullish, she can offset the short futures positions, leaving the calls to make additional profit on the rise of the Nikkei.

This latter strategy will give the hotelier much more flexibility in risk managing her position. It will also not have the disadvantage of causing a loss in the futures markets against the profit of her hotel when it is filled with Japanese tourists. On the contrary, she may even leverage her profits by making an additional profit on the futures market.

Hedging Creatively

In all the examples that we have discussed and investigated, we have always looked at the major hedging requirement of the business concerned. This is very often how businesses that make use of hedging view the facility. A farmer hedges his crop. A miller will hedge the price of the corn, wheat or soybeans he has to buy. Similarly, a business that uses copper in its production process will usually hedge the price of copper.

This is a staid way of looking at hedging. The facility of hedging holds much greater advantage for a business than that mentioned above. We can take any manufacturing firm as an example. Let us assume that the firm manufactures aluminium products, which means it has to purchase aluminium in one form or another. Whichever form it buys it in, the major price determinant of that raw material product will be the price of aluminium. It will therefore be absolutely necessary that the manufacturing firm hedges the price of aluminium. This will go a long way to fixing the cost of its raw material inputs. There may, of course, be other raw material purchasers who should similarly be hedged. There should be an ongoing and constant process of monitoring and hedging of prices of all raw materials that the company requires. This will be the beginning of the gaining of proper control over the cost of production inputs.

The next step of any investigation should be the energy requirements of the firm. Most manufacturing plants have high energy
requirements. Whether they use natural gas, propane, fuel oil or
coal, the hedging of these inputs will play a very important part in
controlling the overheads. In addition to energy used in their manufacturing process, they may run a fleet of motor vehicles. Again the
price of oil, fuel oil or unleaded gasoline will form an important part
of the cost of running the fleet.

The next level of investigation lies in management. The company
will probably make use of financing, usually in more than one form.
Interest rates will therefore play a very important part in the cost
structure of the manufacturing firm. These costs must be monitored
and properly hedged.

The company is also subject and susceptible to changes in the marketplace. In other words, systemic risk will impact on the fortunes of
the business. An investigation should be lodged in order to determine whether the company can hedge itself from time to time
against the impact of these forces.

Just imagine the difference that a hedging policy such as the one
described above would make to the business concern. Budgeting
would become easier and more reliable, while performance forecasts
would improve. The bottom line performance of the company would
show a substantial improvement.

Creative hedging in its first sense therefore means that a business
must look creatively at all its cost elements. Thinking creatively in
this case means that the company must keep an open mind on the
possibilities of hedging a situation that it may not have considered
hedging before. Always ask the question: isn't there some way that I
can get rid of this rogue cost element?

The second sense in which a business must think creatively of
hedging is in being aware of what is happening in the derivatives
market. For example, the energy market in the US is going through
a rapid stage of change, some might say revolution. This will no
doubt be followed by similar developments in Europe. The old
monopolistic system of generating and distributing energy is coming
to an end. Power stations are being privatized. Electricity whole-
salers are mushrooming. New risks, but also new opportunities, are
presenting themselves to wide-awake managers.

People and companies who have never encountered the need or
given the facility for hedging and risk management are now on a
steep learning curve. As a direct result of these privatization developments, the Nymex has, for instance, introduced four new futures
contracts on the distribution of electricity. Both users and suppliers
of electricity are now able to hedge their prices by using futures.
Again, as a direct result of this development the same exchange has

introduced a new futures contract on bulk coal. This is because deregulation is beginning to stimulate competition between power stations. Since most of the electric power in the United States is still generated by burning coal, keen managers are fast realizing the need to risk-manage coal purchases.

It is therefore worth while for all companies that make use of energy – whether in the form of gas, oil or electricity – to be on the lookout for hedging opportunities in this growing market. It is an element of cost that was never hedgeable before in the United States. It is becoming a hedgeable cost input at this stage. The message is to be aware and to keep thinking creatively.

Conclusion

There is a wide and developing world out there. Business and competition is becoming more acute, but also more sophisticated. More and more tools to help risk manage a business are being developed. These tools are there to help and assist businesspeople, but they have to go out and get the knowledge and expertise in order to avail themselves of these facilities. The face of the marketplace is in a state of constant change.

I sincerely hope that the reading of this book has in some way assisted you in gaining a better understanding of what the business of hedging can do for your business. If this understanding adds value to whatever you are doing, it will all have been worth the effort.

INDEX